ANTARCTICA

MAUD   LAND

INDIAN   OCEAN

45°E

AMERICAN HIGHLANDS

POLAR   PLATEAU

90°E

South Pole

Amundsen Dec. 14, 1911

Queen Maud Range

Queen Alexandra Range

ANTARCTIC   MOUNTAINS

WILKES   LAND

*Beardmore
Glacier*

Dry Valleys

ROSS ICE SHELF

*Mt. Erebus
14,450 ft.*

McMurdo
Sound

VICTORIA

LAND

LAND

ROSS   SEA

135°E

BALLENY

ISLANDS

OCEAN

180°

Harold Faye

In memory of my brother, Fairfield

The southern continent has attracted attention from a distance since the time of the ancient Greeks, yet no one had set eyes on it until the nineteenth century. Who in fact saw it first is in dispute, the best-known contenders being a Russian, Thaddeus von Bellingshausen; an Englishman, Edward Brans-field; and an American seal hunter, Nathaniel Palmer. Systematic exploration of the mainland began around the turn of this century.

TRANSANTARCTIC MOUNTAINS, ON THE WAY TO THE SOUTH POLE

WIENCKE ISLAND, BISMARCK STRAIT

The discoverer of Bismarck Strait was Captain Eduard Dallman, who in 1873–74 claimed the islands scattered throughout it for Kaiser Wilhelm of Germany.

ANTARCTICA

FOREWORD BY WALTER SULLIVAN

ELIOT PORTER

E. P. DUTTON   NEW YORK

ACKNOWLEDGMENTS

This book was made possible by a National Science Foundation invitation to photograph in Antarctica. The offer also included provisions for more extensive travel to produce a book.

I wish to thank Guy G. Guthridge, Head, Polar Information Service, National Science Foundation, for reading the manuscript and making very helpful suggestions concerning its accuracy and content. I wish also to express my gratitude to Dr. George H. Denton, University of Maine, for his invaluable advice about places of geological and scenic interest in the dry valleys area of the Transantarctic Mountains; and for reading the manuscript and correcting geological terms and place names. And I am especially indebted to Elise Nobel for her skillful editing and revising of the first draft of the manuscript. Captions have been written by my publisher to offer additional information on the human and natural history of Antarctica.

Published 1978 by E. P. Dutton, a Division of Sequoia-Elsevier Publishing Company, Inc., New York, and simultaneously in Canada by Clarke, Irwin & Co., Ltd., Toronto and Vancouver. All rights reserved under International and Pan-American Copyright Conventions.

Library of Congress Cataloging in Publication Data

Porter, Eliot, 1901–
    Antarctica.

    1. Antarctic regions. I. Title.
G860.P6   1978   919.8'9   78-5784

ISBN: 0-525-05575-4   10 9 8 7 6 5 4 3 2 1   First Edition

Type Composition by Mackenzie-Harris Corp., San Francisco, California. Printed and bound by Dai Nippon Printing Co., Ltd., Japan. Production Director: David Zable. Designed by Eleanor Morris Caponigro.

EMPEROR PENGUINS (*Aptenodytes forsteri*), McMURDO SOUND

CRABEATER SEALS (*Lobodon carcinophagae*), DECEPTION ISLAND

When Deception Island was first sighted in 1820, sealing operations had already killed off the once numerous colonies of seals along the coast of South America, and the same process soon began among the Antarctic islands. The chief victims were the fur seals, desirable for their pelts, and the elephant seal, as a source of oil. Crabeater seals are now believed to constitute about 90 percent of all Antarctic seals, and to number upwards of 30 million.

CONTENTS

TABULAR ICEBERG, GRANDIDIER CHANNEL

Roald Amundsen, the first man to reach the South Pole, gave this graphic account of the nature of icebergs: "The ice barrier is in fact the lip of a gigantic glacier which presses down from the heights of the Antarctic plateau to the sea. This glacier is hundreds of miles in width and between 100 and 200 feet in height. Like all glaciers, at its lower end it is constantly breaking away into icebergs . . ."

COLOR PLATES AND MAPS

STRANDED ICE, LOW TIDE, LITCHFIELD ISLAND

SEA ICE, NEAR THE MINNOWS ISLANDS

FOREWORD

Most people consider exploration of the planet Earth to be complete. To share in the thrill of beholding new landscapes they assume that we can only turn to the moon, Mars, and even more distant bodies of the solar system. Extraordinary feats of space technology—and, in some cases, personal courage—have enabled us to see at close hand the airless surface of the moon, with its bleak, rolling hills under a black sky, or the barren, rubbly surface of Mars.

But there is another "world" on our own planet still only partially explored, where no spacesuits are required—only garments that are especially well insulated. Unlike those celestial realms it is far from lifeless. Yet its landscapes are so alien to those to which we are accustomed that only the cloud formations of the sky seem familiar.

Covering five and a half million square miles, Antarctica contains more than 90 percent of the world's ice and snow. Dry, cold, and windy—frequently gusts exceed one hundred fifty miles per hour—with average winter temperatures of –60°F., the southern continent is nonetheless a land of superb beauty. Whereas the Arctic is an ocean surrounded by great populated land masses—Europe, Asia, and North America—Antarctica is a continent surrounded by the great oceans of the southern hemisphere. It lies beyond the ken of most people because efforts to display, on a flat surface, a map of our spherical planet usually show the Antarctic—if at all—as an irregular ribbon of land in the extreme south.

Some of the ancient Greeks who recognized that the earth is spherical assumed that there must be a continent far to the south to balance the land masses of the north. Early explorers who saw Tierra del Fuego and New Zealand thought they were the northern extremities of a great continent. It was Captain James Cook, in his memorable circumnavigation of the southern seas in the 1770s, who showed that no part of Antarctica reaches into temperate latitudes. If anyone ever penetrates the drifting ice floes to its coast, he said, "I make bold to declare that the world will derive no benefit from it."

Today, with some thirty-five year-round stations being maintained by eleven countries on the continent or its offshore islands, it is clear that the world is, in fact, deriving much benefit from Antarctica. Most of it is in the form of knowledge, such as a broadened understanding of the world's weather, observation of how life can adapt to extreme conditions, and determination of factors controlling ice ages and the radical changes in worldwide sea levels that may occur when large sections of Antarctic ice slip into the sea.

Also looming on the horizon is the possibility that Antarctica may prove to be an important source of fuel, food, and minerals. For many years lead ore has been profitably extracted from east Greenland under conditions comparable to those of Antarctica. It was to some extent the quest for another resource—the fur seals—that led to the first sightings of the continent. Three countries have claimed that their nationals were in the forefront in this regard. The American contender was Nathaniel Palmer, commander of the *Hero*, a small sealing vessel out of Stonington, Connecticut. On November 17, 1820, when he was less than twenty-one years of age, Palmer set forth from Deception Island to seek fresh seal rookeries to the south. (The remarkable nature of Deception Island—a periodically active volcano—is vividly illustrated in this book.) Palmer may have been the first to see the mainland of the Antarctic Peninsula, but the British contend that Edward Bransfield aboard the brig *Williams* did so ten months before Palmer. Bransfield was seeking to establish a British foothold on the south side of Drake Passage, linking the Atlantic and Pacific. The Russian contender as discoverer of the continent was Admiral Thaddeus von Bellingshausen with the ships *Vostok* and *Mirny* on an exploratory venture for the Czar. In 1821 he encountered the *Hero* and young Nat Palmer was invited aboard. The research ship on which Eliot Porter spent much time in preparation of this book was named for that memorable, forty-five-ton sloop.

While the fur seals were being slaughtered by American and British hunters, several expeditions probed towards the main body of Antarctica, including an American one under Lieutenant Charles Wilkes; a French venture led by Dumont d'Urville; and that of Britain's James Clark Ross. It was Ross who, by following the International Date Line south of New Zealand in 1841, entered the largely ice-free sea that bears his name—the most southerly extension of the world's oceans. He sighted the seemingly endless cliffs of the Ross Ice Shelf, barring a sea route to the South Pole and hence called ''The Barrier.'' And he discovered the mighty volcano at McMurdo Sound, which he named for one of his ships: Mount Erebus.

For a half century there was little interest in further exploration, but in 1895 the Sixth International Geographical Congress designated Antarctica the chief remaining challenge to explorers and there ensued the ''heroic era.'' The South Pole was reached for the first time on December 4, 1911, by Roald Amundsen, a month before Robert Falcon Scott's arrival; already weakened (probably by scurvy), Scott's party of five Britons all died on the return journey. A few years later, Ernest Shackleton tried to cross from the Weddell Sea to the Ross Sea but his ship *Endurance* was crushed in the ice, setting the stage for one of the most remarkable feats of survival in modern exploration. In April of 1916, after the loss of the *Endurance*, Shackleton's crew salvaged what provisions they could, including three open boats in which the entire party navigated through the ice floes to Elephant Island—the first land they had set foot on for 485 days. Ernest Shackleton and five of his men then set out in an open whaleboat for South Georgia, eight hundred miles to the northeast, a voyage through gales and pack ice that took fourteen days. After three different vessels had tried and failed, in August 1916 a Chilean ship eventually rescued the men waiting on Elephant Island.

Admiral Richard E. Byrd, Sir Hubert Wilkins, and Lincoln Ellsworth introduced the airplane to Antarctica in the 1920s and 1930s, initiating a succession of American expeditions, several of them led by Byrd. It was, however, the International Geophysical Year of 1957–58 that gave birth to the permanent occupation of Antarctica—as it did to the start of the space age. The bases now there are direct—or indirect—descendents of those set up for that great international effort to understand our planet and its space environment. One was airlifted to the South Pole itself. Others were hauled deep into the interior by Soviet and American tractor trains.

Today the United States spends some fifty million dollars a year to operate its Antarctic bases and support scientists seeking to extract the tantalizing secrets of that land. It was appropriate that the National Science Foundation should turn to one of the great documenters of glorious landscapes and their inhabitants—Glen Canyon, the Adirondacks, East Africa, Baja California, and the like—to record how, and where, that money is being spent. Eliot Porter follows in a noble tradition of Antarctic photography, inaugurated with extraordinary skill and artistry by Herbert G. Ponting, who accompanied Scott's last expedition (though not on the ill-fated trek to the Pole in 1911–12).

Dr. Porter has provided new, glittering perspectives on the continent at the bottom of the world at a time, as he points out, when critical decisions that will determine its future must be made.

WALTER SULLIVAN

INTRODUCTION

Twice as large as Australia, the Antarctic Continent is the last land mass on the planet to be explored. Though not yet developed or exploited, it is nevertheless already threatened by the pursuit of natural riches that human beings have carried on almost since the beginning of their history—not merely to meet their needs but because of an appetite for wealth, the source of power over one's fellow men. Antarctica had escaped the fate of other continents up until modern technology made its penetration possible. But now the tenure of its security in the face of rival national claims appears uncertain.

Already, for example, the Adélie penguins on Cape Royds, whose rookery is the southernmost bird colony in the world, are declining as a result of human disturbance. Since the nineteenth century, as in other parts of the world, the fur seals of the Antarctic have been nearly wiped out by the depredations of sealers; only a few small rookeries have survived. Whales in great numbers and of many kinds once roamed the sub-Antarctic seas; today, because of the efficiency, persistence, and greed of the Japanese, Russian, and Norwegian whaling fleets, among others, they are rarely seen. The blue whale, the largest animal ever to have lived on earth, has been brought near to extermination.

As the pursuit of other species of whales becomes uneconomic because of their scarcity, new targets will no doubt succeed them, including so small an organism as the shrimplike krill, which provides whales and certain species of seals and penguins with their primary sustenance and is the most abundant remaining world resource from which food for human consumption may eventually be processed. Indeed, the killing may have brought about an increase in the abundance of krill, fed as they are by the incredible richness in nutrients and planktonic life of the Antarctic seas. Estimates of the total mass of Antarctic krill vary from several hundred million to several billion tons, from which stock it is proposed that 100 million tons could be harvested annually without depleting the supply.

The exploitation of krill has in fact already begun with the outfitting of several Soviet, Polish, and Japanese trawlers for the purpose. Other nations will soon join the rush and then all hope for restraint in the name of conservation on the basis of sustainable yield, as was the case with the great whales, will be in vain. No Antarctic marine animal commission could be expected to be more successful in controlling the exploitation of these resources than the International Whaling Commission has been in conserving whales. By the time the Antarctic Treaty is susceptible to change in 1991, the pressures to exploit the continent's resources of food, fuel, and minerals may well be irresistible. With the world's population doubling every thirty years, the search for food will become ever more intense, reaching for as yet unexploited sources of animal protein, and for coal, oil, and ore deposits.

As world reserves of oil and gas go on shrinking, and as the richest mineral deposits approach exhaustion, international consortia will begin to exert pressure on governments to permit exploratory drilling in the unglaciated dry valleys (which most geologists believe are unpromising) and on the continental shelf of Antarctica, and to permit intensive exploration of the mountainous regions for ore deposits. Still a formidable obstacle to offshore drilling are the drifting pack ice and icebergs, which could wipe out a drill rig in short order. But although that obstacle may not be surmountable until a technology for underwater drilling has been developed, drilling on land alone will surely and irreversibly change the character of Antarctica. The machinery, the supportive establishments, and the roads that will be necessary for conducting intensive, year-round exploration for oil cannot but produce a devastation at least equal to that for which the consortium of petroleum corporations at Prudhoe Bay on the Arctic coast of Alaska have been responsible. Even were it to be spared the devastation of oil spills, the great, wild, austere beauty of Antarctica will be corrupted by trash and pollution. And oil spills in the Antarctic seas from tankers or wells would have an incalculably damaging effect on Antarctic marine life. Seals, even if not directly injured, could not escape adverse indirect effects; oil-soaked penguins would die by the thousands, and their rookeries would be eventually decimated. These are only the most predictable consequences of economic exploitation of the last untouched land on the planet—the mysterious sixth continent, some of whose unique splendor, both animate and inanimate, is recorded in the pages that follow.

ELIOT PORTER

ANTARCTICA

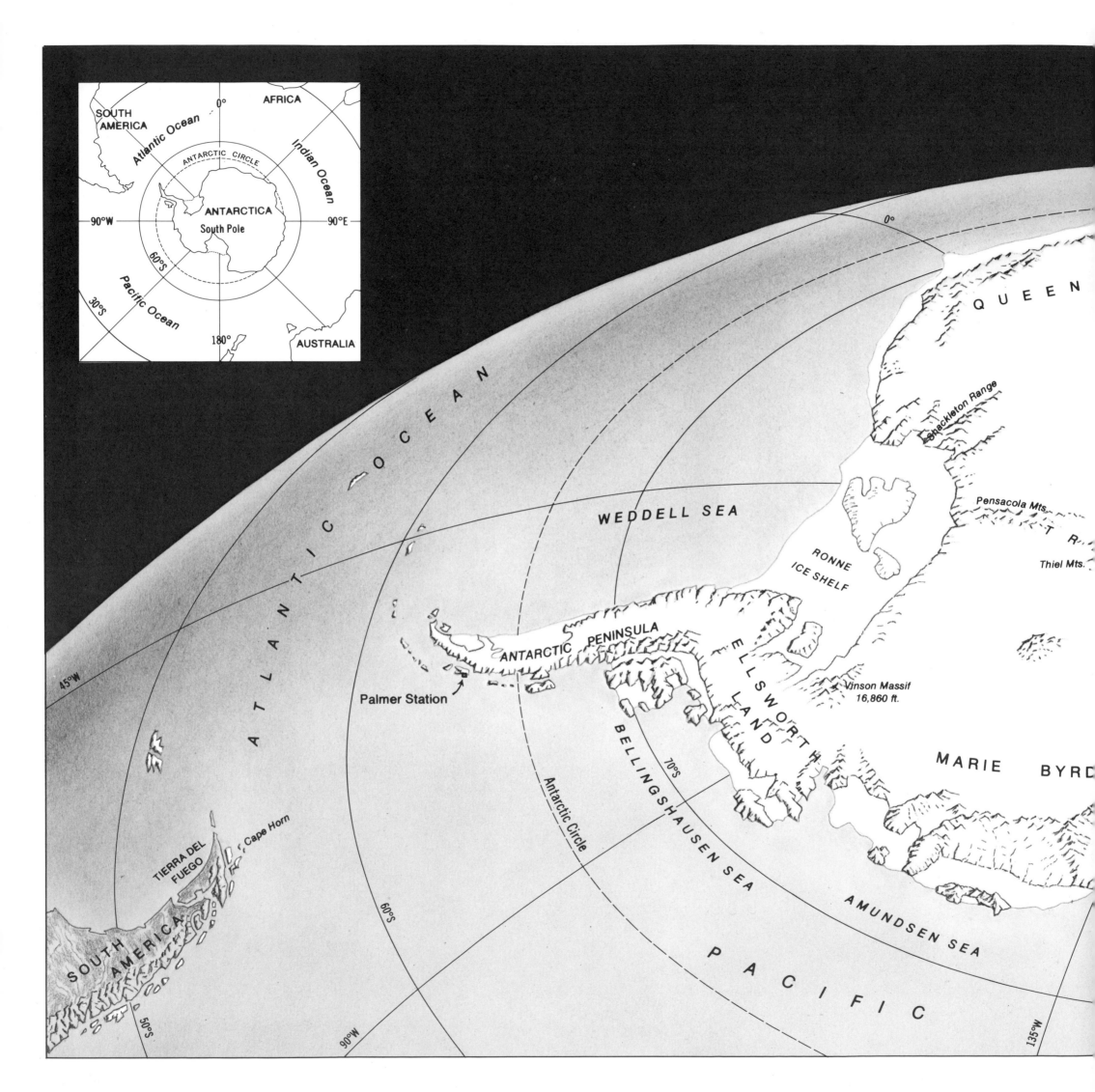

ANTARCTIC CIRCLE

SOUTH
AMERICA
Atlantic Ocean
0°
AFRICA

90°W
ANTARCTICA
South Pole
90°E
Indian Ocean

60°S

30°S
Pacific Ocean

180°
AUSTRALIA

QUEEN

Shackleton Range

Pensacola Mts.

WEDDELL SEA

RONNE
ICE SHELF

T R

Thiel Mts.

ANTARCTIC PENINSULA

ELLSWORTH

Vinson Massif
16,860 ft.

Palmer Station

MARIE BYRD

BELLINGSHAUSEN SEA

LAND

45°W

TIERRA DEL
FUEGO
Cape Horn

Antarctic Circle

70°S

AMUNDSEN SEA

SOUTH
AMERICA

60°S

50°S

90°W

PACIFIC

135°W

A T L A N T I C   O C E A N

ANTARCTICA

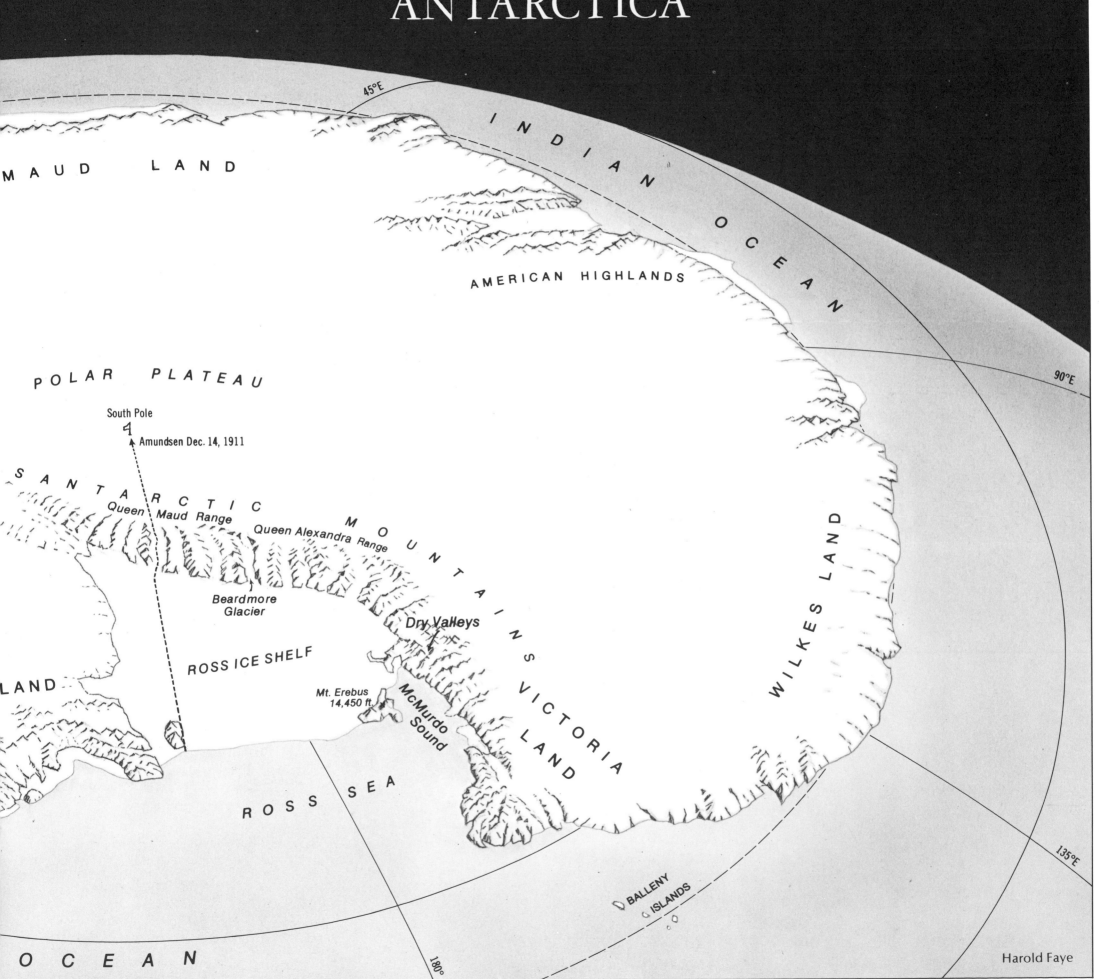

MAUD LAND

INDIAN OCEAN

AMERICAN HIGHLANDS

45°E

90°E

POLAR PLATEAU

South Pole
Amundsen Dec. 14, 1911

A N T A R C T I C

Queen Maud Range

Queen Alexandra Range

M O U N T A I N S

WILKES LAND

Beardmore Glacier

Dry Valleys

ROSS ICE SHELF

Mt. Erebus
14,450 ft.

McMurdo Sound

VICTORIA LAND

...LAND

...LAND

ROSS SEA

135°E

BALLENY
ISLANDS

OCEAN

180°

Harold Faye

I. THE VOYAGE SOUTH

My trip to Antarctica began on a late summer day in Maine. James O. Quinn, who carries the mail to a small group of islands in Penobscot Bay, brought a message that I had had a telephone call from Washington—someone wanting to know whether I would be interested in going to Antarctica. I was not surprised that he had found that out because he is quite used to carrying messages and always tries to get as much information as he can, not only to assist those called but also, I am sure, to satisfy his own curiosity.

Great Spruce Head, the island where I have spent my summers for many years, has no telephone, so I took my boat to our local post office at Sunset, half an hour across the bay, and I called the number in Washington that Quinn had given me. A young woman told me that the National Science Foundation was planning to select painters and photographers to go to Antarctica and record their impressions, and that I was one of a dozen whom they were considering. She asked if I would send some of my work to Washington to help them decide on my qualifications. She said they had already been in touch with my publisher and agent, who were sending them some of my published work.

I had never considered going to Antarctica, a place that seemed to me as remote and unlikely to visit as the moon. However, as time went on I gradually began to get used to the idea; and then I began to worry that it would all turn out to be a false alarm, that I would not be found a suitable candidate and would not be accepted. While I was traveling back to my winter home in New Mexico, I tried to put the whole idea out of my head.

Finally, late in September, the National Science Foundation telephoned. They asked if I thought I could prepare an exhibit of Antarctic photographs for the following September. I said I could. Then they asked if I would be interested in doing a book on the Antarctic. I responded with enthusiasm. Still, it was not clear whether I would go; I would have to wait until the person responsible for making the selections returned from Japan. They said that it would probably be a good idea for me to have the required physical examination done in advance. They would send me the medical forms along with various other documents concerning the Antarctic and a form for clothing measurements.

Holmes and Narver, the contractor for the National Science Foundation, furnishes special cold-weather clothing for all the people sent to Antarctica by the N.S.F. Since all persons going to Antarctica are perforce official visitors, their safety throughout the entire sojourn is the responsibility of the government agency financing it. The fit of all garments, from thermal underwear to down-lined, fur-hooded parka, and including three kinds of footwear—leather boots, mukluks, and insulated white rubber bunny boots—has to be assured before departure. Every person who travels to Antarctica under the auspices of the N.S.F. is also required to attend an indoctrination meeting, at which lectures are given on the vagaries of weather, environmental hazards, and rules for survival under conditions of extreme physical stress and cold or in the event of mishap.

I had my physical exam and filled in my clothing measurements. In late October the National Science Foundation phoned. "You can do either of two things," they said: "join the N.S.F. research vessel *Hero* at Tierra del Fuego or join it at Valparaiso on the way down." They never even said that I had been selected. In early December I was about to fly to Valparaiso when a call came from Washington telling me that the *Hero* had burned out a bearing in her gear box and was being towed to Manzanillo, on the western coast of Mexico. I decided to join her there.

At the Agencia Maritima del Pacifico where the *Hero* was berthed in Manzanillo, I discovered a business-like working vessel, her decks covered with machinery, equipped with winches for trawling, and rigged for sailing with two masts in a compromise style between schooner and ketch. She was much larger than I had expected. A 125-foot ship with a thirty-foot beam, a draft of sixteen feet, and a 600-ton displacement, the *Hero* was crammed with electronic equipment, supplies for a month, and fuel for thirty-two days. Her center of gravity is so low that if she were ever to capsize, she would quickly right herself. Her tough wooden hull is shaped so that in the event of becoming beset in ice, she tends to rise above the water as the pressure against her increases, and thus to escape being crushed.

No one was in sight when I arrived. I shouted, "Anybody aboard?" and presently a slight man with a close-cropped beard appeared. He introduced himself as Captain Lenie. I apologized for my late arrival. He replied that I had arrived in plenty of time before sailing. Several other members of the crew came from below to help with my baggage. I was shown down a steep gangway into the engine room, from which a passage led forward directly into a small general-purpose cabin where several men were sitting around a square table. We were under the midship deck at waterline level. Because the ship is designed for polar seas, there are no port-holes; ventilation is entirely mechanical. As I was soon to discover, in the *Hero* all but a minimum of comfort has been sacrificed to efficiency.

My first impression was of general conviviality, of a well-run ship, with very little personal friction among the members of the crew. I soon felt quite at home, thanks to the informal atmosphere and the cheerfully sardonic manner of the ship's master, Captain Pieter Lenie. It took me a while to learn all their names, but my task was made easier by a list of the ship's complement which was posted in the main cabin.

P. (*Pieter*) J. Lenie, Master
J. (*James*) T. Mosher, First Mate
J. (*John*) T. Folkeinkorn, Second Mate
J. (*John*) Lohr, Radio Operator
R. (*Richard*) F. Parker, Chief Engineer
J. (*John*) Shupe, Assistant Engineer

S. (*Steve*) Kester, Oiler
R. (*Bob*) Rogers, Cook
D. (*Dan*) Reeo, Messman
R. (*Rick*) Benoit, Able Seaman
B. (*Bruce*) Farrow, Able Seaman
J. (*Jim*) McNabb, Common Seaman

During a conversation with Captain Lenie in the common room that night, one of the first things he asked me was how old I was.

I told him, "Seventy-three."

"So you are not the oldest man who has ever been on the *Hero*," he said. "My predecessor was seventy-six."

I wondered at the time what he meant by telling me that. As I got to know him better I realized that he had simply been trying to reassure me that I need not feel self-conscious about my age.

The first mate and second in command, J. T. Mosher, was known to everyone on board simply as Mo. I first met him the morning after I came aboard, when he greeted me on deck with a "Good morning, sir. I hope you will enjoy our ship." His formality did not last long; it couldn't aboard the *Hero*, where everyone was on a first-name basis except with the captain. I guessed that Mo was in his thirties. He was in better physical condition than anyone else on board; lean, well over six feet tall, and evenly tanned from the waist up. To keep fit he exercised regularly on the fantail, doing thirty or forty pushups in all weather. In his left earlobe he wore a thin gold hoop, as a badge of having crossed the equator. His style of dress reflected a flair for the heroic.

His usual costume consisted of tight-fitting black trousers tucked into parachuter's boots, a wide leather belt fastened with a large death's-head buckle which he said was of S.S. vintage, a formidable seaman's knife, and a black pullover sweater. In the tropics he dispensed with the sweater. His stance, legs spread apart, was consistent with his attire, and when he walked he held his arms away from his body, ready for anything.

Mo had been a navigation officer aboard the first United States nuclear submarine to cruise under the ice of the North Pole. On the *Hero* he was responsible for routine navigation. Under ordinary circumstances Captain Lenie took an occasional sight to establish the ship's position and as a check on his officers, but whenever there was sea ice he assumed complete command, steering the ship from the upper bridge, known as the "ice house."

The chief engineer, Richard Parker, was from Tennessee; his assistant, John Shupe, was a Californian. It was difficult to imagine two individuals more different temperamentally and physically. When they appeared together in the cabin, others in the crew often joked that here were Mutt and Jeff. The chief was a tall spare man with a slight stoop that he might have acquired as an accommodation to low bulkhead doors. His speech was relentlessly direct; he did not spare the feelings of those whom he addressed, but his mocking, caustic replies to Shupe's often unguarded remarks were not intended to offend, as one unfamiliar with his sardonic manner might have thought. His bluntness was not unkindness. Parker himself was not quick to take offense or become easily angered; rather, his attitude was that of despairing resignation to the foibles of those for whom he had ultimate responsibility.

Parker was clean shaven and wore his mouse-gray hair long. It hung down on the sides of his aquiline face, covering his ears and the back of his neck. Shupe did not shave, but his beard was not yet very long. It covered his round face below his nose and cheek bones with a thick growth. His hair was curly and matted. Shupe's face came to focus in his nose and mouth like the whiskered muzzle of a small twinkling weasel. His expression, however, was good-naturedly benign. Shupe confessed that at one time he had been much fatter but had recently lost weight. He tried to cut down on his food without much success, failing because he liked too much what he ate. He indulged his appetite not only at meals, but continually during the day, eating the leftover cakes and desserts, which were available at all times to the crew.

Shupe was a remarkably sweet-tempered man; only once or twice did I see him upset by what he complained of as unkind ribbing by Captain Lenie. His equanimity, preserved through all manner of situations relating to personal differences and to mechanical breakdowns, contributed greatly to the atmosphere of congeniality on board. His knowledge of engines and his familiarity with marine equipment, though expressed through a more cheerful disposition, was not less than his chief's. The obvious competence of Shupe and Parker was a major factor in the general confidence that the ship was in good hands.

During our voyage through the tropics, the heat was such that most members of the crew went shirtless during working hours. For the two engineers, Richard Parker and John Shupe, and the oiler, Steve Kester, this was an absolute necessity because the temperature in the engine room was in the high nineties. From time to time during their hours of watch, they would emerge from their hot box to cool off in the forward mess deck cabin, where a small hatch to the deck was kept open. Under the hatch an electric fan sucked in the cooler outside air. It was only at mealtimes that going without a shirt was strictly forbidden, a rule enforced by Bob Rogers the cook and his helper Dan Reeo. Anyone who forgot and came to the table shirtless or barefoot would not be served. When he came forward to escape temporarily from the heat, Parker always carried a greasy white rag slung over his shoulder; he used the rag indiscriminately to wipe the sweat from his face or the grease from his hands or to saw across his back the way one uses a bath towel. Shupe just panted.

With all the hatches and bulkhead doors throughout the ship open, the noise of the engines, generators, and air conditioners filled the common cabin with a throbbing roar. To escape the roar, you could go on deck, which was awash in rough weather, or to the bridge, or you could shut yourself into your own stuffy, inadequately ventilated cubicle. Since the *Hero* had been designed not for the tropics but for Antarctic conditions, the discomforts were greatest in hot weather, and lessened as we entered a cooler zone.

The only member of the crew who was not a professional seaman was the radio operator, John Lohr. His responsibilities were to maintain contact with the National Science Foundation, with the contracting firm of Holmes and Narver, and with the *Hero*'s bases at Ushuaia in Tierra del Fuego and on the Palmer Peninsula, as well as to carry on all other communications that might be required. Lohr was a highly skilled electronics technician and as such was called upon to maintain and repair all other such devices on board the *Hero*, including the gyro compass and automatic pilot. Much of his time aside from all this was devoted to conversation with other members of the fraternity of radio operators, professional or amateur, who are forever seeking other lonely explorers of the ether waves.

I was assigned to one of the three cabins reserved for passengers, along with Bob Pitman, a young ornithological student from San Diego. On the door was a sign reading "Four Scientists—Quatro Scientificos." The other passenger cabins had two berths each. As it happened, Bob Pitman and I were the only passengers—fortunately, since the other cabins and all the space in ours not occupied by our baggage were crammed with ship's supplies that had not yet been stowed. My cameras completely filled the berth above my bed, and the one above Bob's was full of extra blankets and life preservers. The other cabins contained still more blankets and some thirty cases of beer. My tripod stood at the head of my berth, my duffel bag occupied the floor beside it, and Bob's luggage took up all the floor space at his end of the cabin. Later on, when the ship's supplies had been properly sorted and stowed, I was assigned space in the forward laboratory for my photographic gear.

We left Manzanillo on December 9, a day after I boarded the ship. Shortly after six in the evening, we cast off our lines and swung away from the dock, turning toward the harbor breakwater and the open sea. Slowly the ship gained speed, exchanging salutes with a Mexican destroyer that had assisted her into the harbor more than two weeks before. The light of the setting sun still glowed beneath an overcast sky as the *Hero* passed the last headland. She rose and fell slowly, with a gentle rocking motion over the almost invisible Pacific swell; during the three thousand miles of tropical seas that lay ahead I would become so accustomed to that motion that I ceased to be aware of it. We were headed due south toward Easter Island.

I arose early the next morning and went on deck before breakfast to watch the sun rise. After oatmeal, pancakes, and bacon and eggs, I returned to the fo'c's'le deck to see what birds were about. At the start of the voyage, the few that came to investigate our ship, perhaps expecting a handout or some juicy morsel from the cast-out garbage, belonged to the *Sulidae*: red-footed boobies in brown plumage and possibly a few of the hard-to-identify brown boobies. Occasionally a frigatebird sailed by on long black wings, looking for squid or flying fish, which it would snatch from the surface with its long hooked bill. Frigate birds also pirate from the boobies, seizing in midair the fish they have forced them to disgorge. Frigatebirds live a strictly airborne existence in the warm low latitudes, going to land only to breed, once every two years, and never alighting on the sea. Their feathers are oilless and their small, feeble, semi-palmate feet are not adapted for swimming or even for perching, although they do at times rest on the mast tops of ships. Frigate or man-o'-war birds have a higher ratio of wingspread to body weight than any other species in the world, with lightweight, hollow wing bones of great strength.

As we traveled farther south, we began more and more frequently to see storm petrels or Mother Carey's chickens. Throughout the oceans of the world, many kinds of storm petrels occur, each adapted over long periods of evolution to the varying seasons and climates of oceanic islands from the Arctic to the Antarctic. They are among the smallest of oceanic birds; only the diving petrels of the southern hemisphere are smaller. Some ornithologists believe that storm petrels are the most abundant of all birds. The sight of Galapagos storm petrels returning by the millions to their cliffside nests at evening, looking in the distance like a swarm of gnats, led me to concur.

Most storm petrels are dark-plumaged birds with a white rump, strikingly visible at a great distance. Leach's and Galapagos petrels are the common ones encountered in the north and central Pacific. South of the equator Wilson's become the most numerous species. All three are white-rumped birds. Only in the southern latitudes did we begin to see the white-bellied and black-backed storm petrels, both of which have white underplumage.

Petrels feed from the surface of the sea, harvesting the microscopic plankton and small invertebrate organisms that make up the bulk of their diet. They flutter down the sea troughs, thin legs dangling, patting the surface with wide webbed feet as though walking upon it, dancing with the waves as they gather their food. Early mariners called these birds *petrelles*, or Peter's birds, because their behavior suggested St. Peter's legendary walk on the Lake of Gennesareth.

Whereas birds were relatively scarce in these equatorial waters, which are devoid of nutrients, flying fish were fairly common; but one had to be on the lookout for them. Often I was startled by their sudden appearance, thinking as they rose before the bow that what I saw must be some species of sea bird that had been frightened by the approach of the ship. In time, having learned to recognize them at a glance without being fooled, I came to watch for them and would try to discover their method of flight. Flying fish live near the surface of tropical seas; they are slim and torpedo-shaped, somewhat less than a foot long, with large eyes and wide, stiff pectoral fins half the length of their bodies. The blue-gray of their backs, blending with the color of the sea, is a perfect camouflage from above, and their white bellies serve to disguise them against predators from below, whom they evade by escaping above the surface. But near islands, where there are enemies both above and below—frigatebirds in the air, large voracious fish in the water—their existence is a precarious one.

Aboard the *Hero*, I had a close look at flying fish as they emerged from the sea. The pectoral fins extending at right angles to the body acted as airfoils, sustaining glides of many yards before the fish plunged back into the sea. Sometimes I would see clusters of them spring up, fanning out as though in panic to escape pursuit, their white sides flashing in the sun like silvered darts before they splashed down again. A whole school would break the surface of the windswept sea and remain airborne for a distance of more than fifty yards. At such times the fish seemed to rise over the waves, keeping themselves only a little way above the surface. Watching these remarkable aerodynamic feats through my binoculars, I thought I could detect a flutter or vibration of the pectoral fins which would mean that flying fish were not simply passive aerodynes but had made advances in the direction of active sustained flight.

Sometimes a group that had been startled from the water rose all at once, seemingly transformed from a school of fish into a flock of birds. I became obsessed with watching for their instantaneous appearances and disappearances. One night a flying fish landed on deck and I examined its wings. It seemed to me that over eons these long pectoral fins might become wings and that the fish might develop air-breathing equipment, just as the lungfish—for quite different reasons—has developed the ability to live out of water for long periods. The

HERO, RESEARCH SHIP OF THE UNITED STATES NATIONAL SCIENCE FOUNDATION

The hull is of wood, a more flexible material than steel. When beset in ice, its shape allows it to pop up like a pumpkinseed. The Hero is named for the vessel in which Nathaniel Palmer, a nineteenth-century sealing captain from Connecticut, explored Antarctic waters off the South Shetlands. Palmer Station and the Palmer Archipelago are named in his honor.

SUNRISE, SOUTH PACIFIC

WANDERING ALBATROSS (*Diomedes exulans*)

The albatrosses of the world are grouped into thirteen species, of which nine are confined to the sub-Antarctic oceans. Of these all but one (the sooty albatross) belong to the genus Diomedea—*a name given by Linnaeus, who undoubtedly had in mind Diomedes of Greek mythology, whose companions were transformed into birds at his death.*

BEAGLE STRAIT, TIERRA DEL FUEGO

Beagle Strait is named for the vessel made famous by Charles Darwin. Almost a century earlier, the French and British governments both sponsored voyages of exploration into the south seas. The expedition of Captain James Cook in 1772–75 was the first to cross the Antarctic Circle, on January 17, 1773. Cook circumnavigated the Antarctic continent without ever coming within sight of it, and concluded that no such continent existed.

ELEPHANT ISLAND

My first glimpse of Antarctica was this huge island mountain. It was from here, in one of the epic rescues of polar explor-
ation, that in April 1916 Ernest Shackleton and five of his men set out in an open whaleboat for South Georgia, eight hundred
miles to the northeast.

CAPE PIGEONS (*Daption capense*), NEAR GIBBS ISLAND

CHINSTRAP PENGUINS (*Pygoscelis antarctica*) PORPOISING, NELSON STRAIT

NEUMAYER CHANNEL

Icebergs have deluded explorers in search of land at least since Captain James Cook, one of whose officers in December 1772 mistook the sight of one for the mainland of Antarctica. Later, he wrote in his journal that icebergs "are now become so familiar to us that our apprehensions are never of long duration and are compensated by the very Curious and Romantik Views these ice islands frequently exhibit."

ADÉLIE PENGUINS (*Pygoscelis adeliae*), TORGERSEN ISLAND

For the Adélie penguins—and the two other common species of Antarctica, the gentoos and chinstraps—the tail is a bristly, stubby appendage that keeps the bird from falling over backward, functioning rather in the manner of a third leg. Its feather shafts are exceedingly stiff with very much reduced barbs and vanes, similar to the stiff feathers in the tail of a woodpecker, which support it in a vertical position against a tree trunk. At first glance, the triple print left by a penguin suggests the print left by a small, cloven-hoofed animal walking a direction opposite to the one actually taken by the bird.

GERLACHE STRAIT

This strait, like so many geographical features of the Antarctic, is named for the man who explored it—Lieutenant Adrien de Gerlache de Gomeny, a Belgian who in 1898 made several landings here, collecting plant and animal specimens and recording data on glaciers and geological formations. In the Bellingshausen Sea, Gerlache's ship, the Belgica, *was beset in pack ice and drifted for over a year, so that the expedition became the first to winter in the Antarctic.*

MOSS AND LICHENS, SHORTCUT ISLAND

In 1895 an ordinary seaman, Carsten Borchgrevink, on a Norwegian expedition sponsored by Svend Foyn, the inventor of the harpoon gun, discovered pale-green lichens growing on the rock of an offshore island in the Ross Sea. This was the first indication that there was anything growing on the Antarctic mainland.

WHALEBONES, PORT LOCKROY, ANTARCTIC PENINSULA

The first land-based whaling station in the Antarctic was established by a Norwegian, Carl Anton Larsen, on South Georgia Island in 1904. This marked the beginning of systematic whaling in the region, although largely unsuccessful attempts to hunt whales there had begun some decades before. By 1930, when over 40,000 whales were killed and processed—either in stations like the one at Port Lockroy or entirely aboard factory ships—the numbers of whales were already dwindling. An International Agreement for the Regulation of Whaling, signed by nine nations in 1937, supposedly put a curb on the slaughter—although in the following year a record total of 46,039 whales were killed.

MORNING LIGHT, GERLACHE STRAIT

flying fish seemed to be moving in an evolutionary direction opposite to that of certain avian polar species. Penguins have lost the power of flight entirely; and heavy birds such as murres and puffins seem to avoid flying as much as possible because they have to work so hard to remain airborne. Flying fish might, I thought, become birds that returned to the sea to breed, just as penguins, birds that have become fishlike, return for that purpose to the land.

The December days slipped past unmarked by distinguishing events, losing their identity in the cycle of shipboard routine. A moderate wind blew endlessly from the same easterly quarter. I saw a flashing sunrise on a windswept sea. I watched for the birds that rarely appeared over the sterile subtropical wastes. The surrounding horizon, its monotony unchanging despite the constant, undulating rise and fall of the waves, was mesmeric in the drowsy hours of midday; and the day's end brought a glint of flying fish, the glow of sunset clouds, and then sudden darkness.

But minor events that in other circumstances would have passed almost unnoted made certain days memorable. One morning a small land bird was observed on board. No one had seen it come. At first it kept to the rigging and the highest parts of the superstructure, but as it gradually became used to the crew it alighted on deck and began to forage about, pecking at the hawsers and stopping frequently to investigate puddles of salt water. It seemed tired. Thinking it might be thirsty, Shupe put out a bowl of water, but either Shupe was wrong or the bird simply failed to recognize the water for what it was. Before the day ended the little visitor had become very tame; once in its constant foraging it alighted on my foot. From its streaked sides, brownish-gray back, faint wingbars, and lemon-yellow rump, it appeared to be either an immature or a female of the genus *Dendroica*—a myrtle or an Audubon's warbler. Some of the crew tried to feed it, but, being an insectivorous bird, it was not interested in the bread crumbs they scattered on deck. This little warbler, so out of its element at sea, must have been blown off shore by the easterly wind. The last time I saw it was in the evening as it flew back and forth along the starboard alleyway between the fo'c's'le and fantail. The next morning it was gone. During the night it had valiantly flown on in search of a land a thousand miles to the east.

At sea, the best time is the beginning of the day. Almost every morning I rose before the sun and went on deck to watch the break of day. I usually made my way to the bridge where I would find the first mate, Mo, on watch. He too preferred the early hours, and told me that he liked to see the world change as the sun came up. At these times he would talk of his experiences and aspirations, and of the places he liked best. Among these was the coast of Maine, a preference that established a bond between us. While we talked, the dark of night gradually retreated, giving way to a uniform grayness that was often the precursor of some of the most beautiful chromatic spectacles anywhere on earth. Though many times the day broke drab, with a cloud cover too dense for the sun to penetrate, on several occasions we were rewarded for our persistence. Sometimes after a night of rain, when a change of weather was imminent, and the strong winds of the day before had been replaced by gentle easterlies that calmed the sea without dispersing the cloud cover, the sun would rise out of the ocean orange-red only to disappear behind low clouds. Then it would not be seen again until it had risen high above the horizon, by then a dazzling white.

One day in the southern dog latitudes, I went on deck well before sunrise, knowing that dawn breaks rapidly in the tropics. The sea was an oily calm with a long, low Pacific swell. The *Hero* rose and fell gently. At first only a faint brightening showed on the eastern horizon, but then the morning twilight rapidly enveloped the entire sky in a greenish glow. The light radiated uniformly over a wide arc until, as I watched, the horizon at one single point caught fire. Where the sun ignited the fringes of the lowest and most distant clouds, flames leaped up. The intensity of the conflagration grew; cloud after cloud burst into flame. Rays of light spread in a fan above the distant fire—a display that was in fact a negative composed of the shadows cast by the horizon clouds on the mist and haze within the lower atmosphere. The beams of light all pointed down to a place as yet out of sight. I waited as the display intensified, impatient for its culmination and yet wishing it would never end. Then without warning—indeed to my intense surprise—the limb of the sun, the focal point of the display, sprang forth as though released by a spring. It thrust suddenly through the elastic barrier of the atmosphere, materializing from nothing into a substantial slice, and from then on the advance seemed to slow, as though it no longer had to push with such force. I had the distinct impression of the momentary release of greenish light. Was this the legendary green flash at sunrise?

As the day advanced, the horizon continued to be rimmed with clouds; overhead was clear blue sky. A stiff wind rose out of the southeast. The sea shimmered in the morning sun, each whitecapped wave set off with a myriad of tiny mirrors that shifted and changed position as they reflected the sun, giving to the surface of the sea in the quarter towards the sun the coruscating glitter of a woven metallic fabric.

The sea had seemed to change color as we moved south from temperate latitudes through the tropics and into southern waters. From the very first days of the voyage I had been taking note of the color of the ocean water. It seemed to me that, unlike the North Atlantic, with which I had become familiar through many summers along the coast of Maine, the Pacific off the Mexican coast was clear and unturbid, probably because it had been less polluted by industrial wastes and river sediments. At first it had appeared to be a deep cerulean blue, a reflection of the sky. This hue had changed to a deep purple-blue, which made me think of the Mediterranean, or more precisely the Aegean of classical times, described by the Greeks as "wine-dark." Purple grapes could produce a wine of this Pacific color. The only other Pacific water I knew was the sea around the Galapagos Islands. There the water was richer, for the Humboldt Current carried nutrients from the ocean depths, as well as lime sediments from the marine life of the islands' shores. The lime turns sea water a pale, milky greenish blue, in the same way that colloidal minerals give glacial streams their milky blue character. The sea around the Galapagos Islands was therefore an aquamarine, in contrast to the open ocean's purple-blue.

On this particular morning the sea had undergone another change. I noticed that the blue was darker, almost an ultramarine, which seemed tinged with red. The contrast gave the sky near the horizon a particularly striking greenish cast. Even towards the zenith, where its hue was deeper, the contrast was still noticeable. The wind was so gentle that I could study the reflecting planes on the small waves' inner surfaces, and I saw that they were in fact violet; it was this color that gave the water its reddish cast. Still smaller facets of the wavelets reflected the sky and were greener than the rest of the water's surface. These smallest facets generally took the form of a double arc, like the wings of a bird, as a consequence of the dynamics of wavelets and the way they are blown up by the wind. Thus, three colors combined to produce the characteristic color of the sea: the purple depths below the reflecting surface, by far the largest area; then the lighter violet planes of semireflected light; and last the greener hue of the tiny wavelet facets. Taking the ocean as a whole, I now began to make out its true color as distinctly and strongly violet: a violet sea. From whatever side of the ship I observed it the color remained the same. At first I thought the color might be accounted for by a reflection of sky that enhanced the inherent blueness of the water; but when, in the afternoon, with clouds building up to the point of almost complete coverage of the sky, the violet remained, I felt sure that it must be inherent. Where the sun shone between the clouds on the water, streaks of a lighter violet were plain.

On another day the sun rose at six. The cumulus clouds around the horizon floated above the sea, with shafts of rain visibly descending from their dark lavender undersides; their towering tops were illumined as the sun rose behind more distant clouds, the first faint pink turning to orange, yellow, and gold. The sunlight streaked across the sky, catching the clouds to the west full on and stippling those to the east with spots of light.

The most beautiful sunrises and sunsets occurred in the low southern latitudes, where the moist atmosphere favored cumulus cloud formations, producing spectacular displays that opened and closed the day. At dawn the horizon was rimmed with discrete clouds anchored to the sea by trailing veils of rain while overhead all was clear. To us on board it seemed that the *Hero* moved within an enchanted inviolate space; but this was an illusion, for the clouds were in fact evenly distributed, appearing to be more closely packed only when viewed at an angle.

Sometimes I lay on the main hatch cover where I was safe above the seas that washed through the scuppers and surged across the deck with each heavy roll of the ship. As I lay on my back with my eyes shut and the sun full on my face, the light that filtered through my lids was yellow, tinged with pink, and when I squeezed them tight it became deep red from the blood they contained. By concentrating on the space below the lighted background of my eyelids I became aware of ghostlike gray objects that seemed free-floating yet subject to some degree of control by eye motion. These ghosts were filamentous objects, fragments, or better, shadows of long since disused capillaries, the remnants of embryonic structures. In a sense I was looking into my past.

Bob Pitman, the young ornithologist from San Diego, stayed on deck with his notebook and binoculars during all daylight hours. He was good at identifying birds and I learned a lot from him. A part of his work involved collecting specimens by shooting any bird that ventured too close to the ship—an activity whose scientific value escaped me, since the great majority of the birds he shot had been positively identified before they were taken.

Below the roaring forties of the far South Pacific, as we approached Cape Horn, flocks of whalebirds, known also to mariners as icebirds, would circle the *Hero* for minutes on end. The whalebirds are small blue petrels of the genus *Prion*. They are unlike other small petrels in the delicate shading of their gray, blue, and white plumage, and have a distinctive black line through the eye. For the first observers of their pale plumage in the stormy Antarctic sea, the birds appeared to have an affinity with ice and were thus called icebirds. When, after several misses, Bob Pitman succeeded in bringing one of them down, because of its camouflaging color he lost sight of it in the rough sea and never recovered it, despite repeated circling by the *Hero*. He wounded a second whalebird, which fell fluttering to the surface of the water, where its pitiful struggles attracted other birds of its own species. One of these alighted beside it and was also shot, after which to my relief the others were frightened away. Although I saw in their behavior a touching concern for the welfare of a companion, or at least a curiosity about it, the ornithologists' explanation is that other prions were attracted to what appeared to be a feeding bird. When the two dead whalebirds were brought on deck they proved bigger than they had appeared in flight. I was able to examine at first hand the curious tubular nostrils that characterize the large order to which they belong, and the baleenlike fringes that border their bills, used for sifting plankton from sea water. When Bob said, "Aren't they pretty?", I restrained myself from answering that they were— but how much less so than the living bird.

Below the Tropic of Capricorn, birds became more plentiful. Shearwaters of several kinds came circling towards the ship, inspected it, and were off again. The majority came from the starboard quarter, slanting across our bow on stiff wings, tilting this way and that so as to present now their dark backs, now their white breasts and dark-bordered underwings as they dipped and glided into the troughs of waves. In wind and rain and spray these birds were completely at home. New kinds of petrels, belonging to the genus *Pterodroma*, also appeared. Although larger than the storm petrels, because of their relatively small size and their mothlike swarming congregations, they have been named gadfly petrels. Probably the species of *Pterodroma* we saw most often was Cook's petrel, a dark-backed bird with light underplumage, common in the southeastern Pacific.

Christmas Day found us well into the southern latitudes. It was a cool, blustery day with the highest seas yet, forewarnings of what lay ahead. The long ocean swells advancing from the southwest appeared to be more than a hundred feet from crest to crest. The height of these waves was of course not easy to estimate without exaggerating; but from the midship deck they towered high above me, shutting out any view of the sea beyond. They came in groups of four and five, with smaller waves in the stretches between, and as they slid beneath the *Hero* they barely caused her to list while she rose on their smooth sides.

To celebrate Christmas, Bob Rogers had cooked a feast, beginning with hors d'oeuvres that used up the last of the fresh celery and concluding with two pies and a pink cake. At midday I telephoned my family in Santa Fe by means of ham radio connections. Aside from many such phone calls and the holiday menu, Christmas on the *Hero* passed unobserved.

In the windy forties I saw my first wandering albatross, the largest species of the genus *Diomedea*. The bird was discovered following the *Hero* on the morning of December 28, having attached itself to her wake sometime during the night. Soon it was joined by a second bird. Both wore the plumage of juveniles, with dark backs and wings, their breasts and wing linings mottled brown and white. As the male wandering albatross matures, in a process that takes several years, his head and body become progressively whiter until only the upper surfaces of his wings remain black. As he tilts away exposing his snowy underside one can see his black-tipped white underwing lining with its narrow, trailing black margins. The wandering and royal albatrosses both attain a wingspread of eleven and a half feet, greater than in any other living species. Indistinguishable from one another in flight, these are the great albatrosses of legend, as distinct from the smaller species that are grouped together by sailors under the name of mollymauks.

The two immature birds that followed the *Hero* were masters of soaring and gliding flight. Most of the time they remained astern, swinging from side to side across our wake, ever on the watch for some edible morsel. Albatrosses must have learned from long experience, going back to the time when the first sailing vessels entered the southern seas, that ships offer a potential bonanza. When our breakfast garbage was dumped that morning both albatrosses settled on the surface in the litter to pick it over and were soon lost to sight far astern, to reappear some time later.

The albatross is a magnificent bird whose dimensions, considering its oceanic life, appear quite unlikely. The short, thick, heavy body and disproportionately large bill, bluish in juveniles but becoming pink with maturity, do not suggest compatibility with long sustained flight. In fact, however, the extremely long and narrow wings provide in even moderate winds the lift necessary to keep the heavy bird airborne. As it flies, the albatross's supremacy as a creature adapted to the wind and the sea is immediately manifest. The bird sustains a gliding flight for hours at a time, with hardly a flap of the wings. In the albatrosses that circled our ship, advancing before and falling behind it, the wing movements were undetectable. Now rising high above the surface, now skimming just above the waves, tilting on edge as the wind demanded, often with the down wing scarcely missing the water, they followed the contour of each wavelet by the most sensitive adjustments, never quite touching the water. Automatically responding to a gust of air, they would turn to present the other wing to the surface in a new tack. Although they could alight on the sea with perfect grace and ease, to arise again, except in the face of a strong wind, required much paddling with their great webbed feet.

Wandering albatrosses head for land only once a year to breed, spending the rest of their lives at sea, following the stormy westerlies and thus quite probably circumnavigating the globe. They nest on sub-Antarctic islands where each pair raises a single chick. Throughout the austral summer the chicks are fattened on regurgitated food; when winter comes the young birds, by then as large as the adults but still clothed in infant down, are deserted by the parents. Through the cold months of snow and freezing temperatures the young albatrosses sit hunched on their nests burning stored body fats for warmth and the slow transformation from infant down to adult plumage. With the advent of spring the young birds begin to exercise their wings and on the return of the parent birds to the nesting colony, after months of abandonment, they are at last unceremoniously pushed out of the nests to make way for a new generation. For another year the young birds remain in the vicinity of the nesting island, learning to fend for themselves before they take up a life of wandering across the pan-Antarctic ocean.

From the day we first sighted the wandering albatrosses they followed us constantly. The farther south we went the more numerous they became. Two species of the smaller albatrosses or mollymauks also appeared. There were many of the black-browed and a few of the gray-headed species. The black-broweds did not seem to take the same interest in the *Hero* as the wanderers, following us less persistently and circling at a greater distance. I got the impression too that they were swifter birds. The name of the black-browed albatross refers to a black line above the eye which can be seen only at close range. Nevertheless, the species is readily distinguishable from other mollymauks by its white head, and is recognizable at a great distance. As it glides on edge, its back facing you, you can see the pure white body and the long black wings extended out at right angles. On the reverse tilt the underside of the bird comes into view to reveal a white band extending the length of the black-bordered wings.

Towards the end of December we began to approach the southern coast of South America. The weather was now much more boisterous than before. We encountered intermittent pockets of sea fog and low scudding clouds, bringing with them rain, stiff winds, and rough seas. Birds of many kinds became much more numerous. There were shearwaters, giant petrels, and storm petrels, as well as the ubiquitous albatrosses, and I now saw diving petrels for the first time. As small as storm petrels, they are completely unlike them in flight and feeding habits. They fly like the auklets and murrelets of the northern hemisphere, on frantically whirring wings, and instead of fluttering over the surface to scoop up food as storm petrels do, they plunge in after it. When I first saw this happen I was very much taken aback, having expected a more ternlike diving behavior. Diving petrels frequently rest on the sea, a habit not usual for storm petrels, and from this position they either dive directly or rise quickly on their whirring wings and suddenly plunge into the water, to disappear without alighting again.

When we had come within fifty miles of the Chilean coast, still invisible behind the rain clouds and fog but detectable on the ship's radar, we began to see Magellanic penguins, recognizable by their striped faces—single individuals at first and then small groups of them. I was surprised to encounter penguins so far from land; but, as they are accomplished swimmers either on or under the surface, the distance gave them no difficulty. Probably they had ventured that far in search of food that could be pursued without risk; in those latitudes the only predators they had to fear would have been occasional killer whales. Sitting high on the surface they appeared as buoyant as ducks yet they could submerge as inconspicuously as grebes.

Our first sight of land was the tiny Ildefonso islands sixty miles west of Cape Horn—a group of barren, forbidding rocks that take the full force of westerly gales and the mountainous seas of the Drake Passage. Our course continued east, leaving Horn Island to port, and then turned due north to enter the Beagle Channel. I was asleep when we passed Horn Island light at 2:30 A.M. Atlantic time. I awoke at seven and went on deck, to find several islands with high rounded profiles—the tops of mountains—in sight ahead to port and starboard, and a small one to starboard a few miles astern. On the horizon, away off to the left below a layer of low-hanging clouds, I saw what looked like sunlit cliffs. Seen through binoculars they turned out to be snow-covered mountain peaks. These were the mountains on Hoste Island, the largest land area south of Beagle Channel.

The islands we were approaching, Lennox to port and New Island to starboard, were sere and brown, treeless but covered with grass and bushes. From the shore the land rose abruptly in eroded cliffs and steep moorlike slopes. Their desolation was intensified by lowering clouds and bright gaps where the sun, low in the east, struggled vainly to break through. The sea around us was flecked with whitecaps raised by a stiff, cold west wind that only added to the cheerlessness of the scene. We were accompanied by a wheeling congregation of giant petrels and skuas, our companions from the open ocean. It was cold and I soon sought the shelter of the bridge.

As we drew closer to Lennox and New islands, a white line of waves breaking on their exposed beaches and promontories confirmed the impression of inaccessibility and isolation. At higher elevations I could see a different kind of vegetation from that of the moorland slopes. From a distance it appeared smooth, dark, and mosslike, but as we approached I realized that the dark mass was made up of treetops; I was looking at a primeval forest. At its lower limit a wall of bleached and twisted trunks stood out like tangled fibers of frayed rope. These were the noted evergreen beeches of Tierra del Fuego. Along the shores of the islands, above the level of high tide, rocks were splashed with orange lichens, and in gullies on seaside cliffs, sediments had been exposed in a profusion of colors, ranging from purple to the rich browns of iron oxide.

All around us were Magellanic cormorants, hurrying in different directions on fast-beating wings, in groups of three or four or as many as twenty. With white throats and underparts they are quite different from the all-black double-crested cormorants of the North Atlantic. The Magellanic cormorants also display flashing white specular patches on their wings as they fly.

Two black-backed kelp gulls, evidently considering the *Hero* a good bet for a handout, circled us expectantly. Bob Pitman threw out some frozen fish he had been saving for bait, towards which they instantly plummeted before the slower giant petrels could maneuver about. Their success was short-lived, however; a savage attack in the air by two skuas soon forced them to drop the fish. One gull retrieved its fish in midair only to lose it again to another skua.

We anchored off a beach on Picton Island, where a somber forest of beech trees, their trunks bleached and contorted by the wind, grew down to the very edge of the gravel. After waiting half a day for the arrival of the Argentine pilot—whose presence was merely a formality intended to support his government's claim of sovereignty in these coastal waters—we received a wireless message directing Captain Lenie to proceed down the Beagle Channel, where the pilot boat was having engine trouble. Near the settlement of Harborton we sighted a P.T. boat bringing the pilot. He came aboard the *Hero*, and we were on our way to Ushuaia, its base in South America.

The Beagle Channel probably originated as a rift in the continental crust that opened millions of years ago, when the separation of South America from Africa and Antarctica was in its early stages. At that time the

Andes, the longest mountain range in the world, were being upraised. Beyond their terminating point in Tierra del Fuego, they drop beneath the surface of the South Atlantic. Here the chain continues as a submarine plateau, the Scotia Ridge, which in its turn connects South America with the Antarctic Peninsula. Some geologists suggest that the mountainous Antarctic Peninsula is in fact a re-emergent southernmost extension of the Andes.

On the eastern extension of Tierra del Fuego, just before the Andes are submerged to become the Scotia Ridge, the mountains are no more than low wooded hills, whereas those farther to the west reach a height of four thousand feet, well above tree line, and are capped with snow. Still farther west, on the Chilean peninsula of Tierra del Fuego, is the Cordillera Darwin, whose still more formidable peaks ascend to seven thousand feet and are encased in glaciers.

As we approached Ushuaia, bucking a stiff west wind, lenticular clouds filled the evening sky. It was January 2, and the southern summer was at its height; but darkness had fallen before the lights of Ushuaia appeared, miles ahead off the starboard bow. At such a time, a small town's lights give an exaggerated impression of size. Those of Ushuaia, distributed along the waterfront for several miles, further enhanced this effect. Ushuaia had been founded in 1869 by English missionaries, and from what I had read, I had expected it still to be a pioneer village, even though I had been told that it boasted a population of 3,500, and of being the world's southernmost city of that size. I did not find it an attractive city. In many respects it is like a pioneer town or a mining camp, with shoddy construction and unplanned, disorderly growth. In other respects it is a town overwhelmed and cheapened by a tourist invasion for which it was unprepared.

Ushuaia is built along the shore of a sweeping bay, on a sloping strip of land not more than half a mile wide. Behind it a mountain range ascends steeply to an altitude of four thousand feet, providing a dramatic background to the city. The land it occupies was originally covered with a dense forest of evergreen beech that extended down to the water. It has been gradually cleared over the years to a distance of three-quarters of a mile. Beyond the forest edge, with its advancing regrowth of small trees, the mountainsides are clothed with beeches of increasing size up to a sharply delineated tree line above which only alpine vegetation grows, and where the terrain is all gravel talus, rock cliffs, and snowbanks.

Along the shore as we approached we had seen many places where the forest had been cleared by burning, the quickest and cheapest way to remove trees, to provide grassland for sheep ranching, the principal husbandry of the region. As the population increases, the forest resources of Tierra del Fuego are being treated with less abandon and logging is replacing burning as a less wasteful way to clear land.

With the *Hero* scheduled to sail as soon as provisioning was completed, I had a few days to see something of Tierra del Fuego. On the day after our arrival I followed a trail up the mountain through the beech forest to a high valley. I left right after lunch with my camera on my back and tripod in hand and returned just before supper. The unaccustomed exercise after a sedentary month at sea gave me such stiff muscles that the next day I went nowhere and occupied myself with photographing dolphin gulls as they scavenged refuse on the pier. After that I hired a car and driver as the best way of seeing more of the country.

Bob Pitman had left the *Hero* at Ushuaia, and two days before we sailed on January 8, two groups of scientists with N.S.F. grants for Antarctic research arrived from Buenos Aires. Also joining the ship was Robert Dale, special projects manager for N.S.F. polar operations, who was on an inspection trip to Palmer Station. All day on January 8 we waited for the Argentine pilot and at four o'clock he finally appeared. The light of evening was fading as the *Hero* steered south past New Island for the Antarctic Peninsula, six hundred miles away.

The Drake Passage, the wide strait between South America and Antarctica that we were now entering, is reputed to be the stormiest and most dangerous stretch of the southern ocean. As the circumpolar current is funneled through it, driven by perpetual westerlies, the waves build up to unprecedented heights. Fifty-foot waves are not uncommon and others reaching a hundred feet are not unknown. Secretly I was half hoping for rough weather so that I could photograph green water breaking over the bow of the *Hero*. By morning, when we were eighty miles east of Horn Island, a westerly gale was indeed blowing, kicking up much white water and raising a considerable sea. Running in the trough, the *Hero* rolled much more than she had on the voyage south, and on the big waves she listed as much as thirty degrees to each side. Of the eight scientists on board— young men most of them—only two turned out for breakfast; all the rest were seasick.

By the next afternoon we were well into the Drake Passage. The wind had dropped, promising a calm sea on the morrow. Three of the five days of the *Hero*'s provisioning at Ushuaia had been sunny, warm, and windless. It appeared that we were still under the influence of the summer weather pattern of Tierra del Fuego.

The sun rose on January 10 over a shining sea. The polished metallic surface undulated to the ground swell in such a way as to suggest a loosely stretched film billowed from underneath by a current of air. We were lifted again and again by especially large hills of water which could best be understood as the result of a complicated system made up of two or more swells moving in different directions, now interfering with and now reinforcing one another. These systems could be distinguished from the vantage point of the ice house.

An immature wandering albatross circled the ship for hours, keeping always close to the surface where weak updrafts of air produced by the swells were just sufficient to support its gliding flight. A black-browed albatross circled too but could maintain a greater height because of its small size. It frequently turned on edge, one wing skimming the surface—its customary manner of flight under windy conditions. Wilson's petrels were abundant and two larger petrels came by, both with white rumps; one was black-bellied with gray, longitudinally striped wings, and the other was white-bellied and dark on top. Flocks of prions appeared but no cape pigeons yet. This quiet sea was the fearful Drake Passage! Although we had not yet crossed the line of convergence between the cold waters of the Antartcic and the warmer waters of the southern hemisphere, we were now more than halfway to our destination.

II. PALMER STATION AND THE ISLANDS

My first glimpse of Antarctica came on January 11, when an outpost of the South Shetland archipelago appeared off the port bow. During the night we had crossed the Antarctic Convergence to enter a new climatic zone. From then on weather conditions would be controlled by all the vagaries of unpredictable forces originating on the Antarctic Continent—which even in summertime can bring fierce sudden gales, days gloomy with driven snow, or ice fogs and whiteouts. Yesterday's calm had been replaced by wind and low stormy clouds racing across the sky. On our left rose Elephant Island, a huge, menacing mountain hulk, all ice, snow, and rock shrouded in shifting clouds through which there was an occasional glimpse of a sunlit glacier. It was on this dour, inhospitable point of land that Shackleton's crew took refuge after the *Endurance* was crushed by ice in 1915.

For me that morning was the beginning of an entirely new experience. The Antarctic was as different from Tierra del Fuego as Tierra del Fuego had been from Manzanillo. A harsh desert land of ice-encased mountains, of the flightless penguin and hardy pelagic birds, of seals and whales, Antarctica is a region where man's presence has been minimal, where he never ventured and could not survive before he was able to bring with him, by means of his technology, enclaves of the temperate climate of his origin. But for all its grim and hostile character, Antarctica with its pristine snows, its unbelievable clarity of air, and its blue, cascading ice is sublimely beautiful.

At Gibbs Island, the next of this northern group, thirty miles south of Elephant Island, the geologists were to be set ashore for three weeks' exploration and paleomagnetic measurements. Much smaller than Elephant Island, Gibbs is a ten-mile-long ridge of mountain peaks that project above the Antarctic Sea as though by accident. For the first time flights of cape pigeons, recognizable by their black and white spotted wings, wheeled past us in formation; and we also came across small numbers of chinstrap penguins. We circled the eastern end of the island, drawing in close to the south shore in search of a good landing place. Hundreds of penguins now came out to inspect us, swimming rapidly alongside the ship in their curious, looping, porpoiselike way, in and out of the water very much as though they were flying. While a party went off in a Zodiac—an inflated rubber landing craft—to look for a landing place, the penguins continued to play around the ship, splashing and floating on their backs to preen. In many places the glaciers that nearly cover Gibbs Island flow down to the water's edge, where they end as blue, crevassed ice cliffs, the source of icebergs. Wherever the rock slopes are bare, chinstrap penguins have taken possession, so completely in some spots that it is difficult to walk between the nests. The population of penguins on Gibbs Island must be in the millions.

I went ashore with the first boatload of the geologists' supplies in order to have as much time as possible for photography. In a half-sheltered cove whose smooth black boulders were slippery with algae, landing between one wave and the next with quantities of equipment was a hazardous business, which luckily this time went without mishap. The geological party had decided to set up camp on a more or less level shoulder unoccupied by the birds, where mosses grew in a thin, closely woven carpet. Here also a muddy orange lichen covered the exposed sides of the larger boulders. On that gray, blustery day Gibbs Island was a forbidding place whose grimness was only infrequently relieved as the sun broke through gaps in the clouds to create a momentary oasis of light. Without warning the dark clouds would close in again, bringing snow flurries on

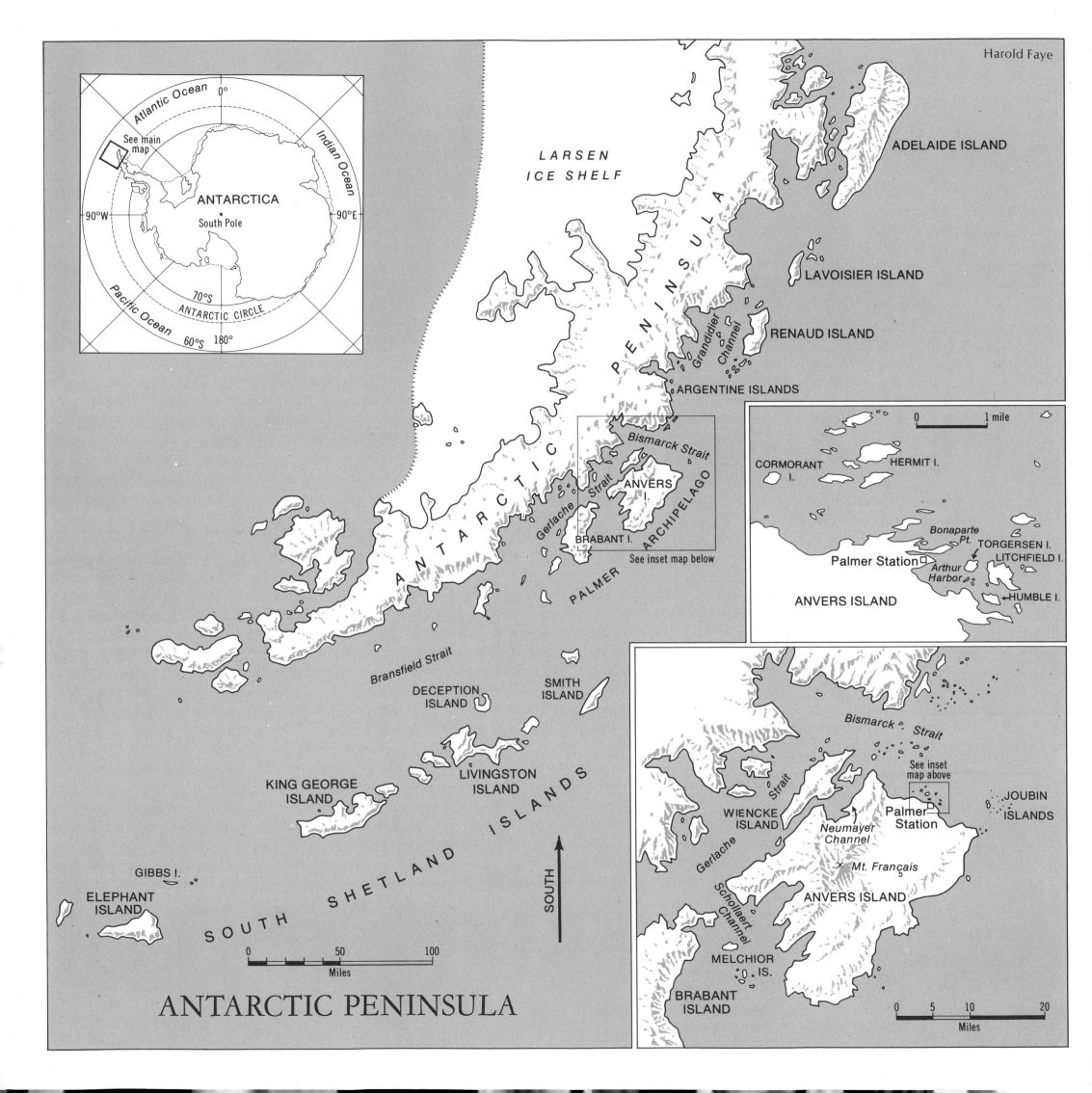

Harold Faye

Atlantic Ocean
0°

See main map

Indian Ocean

ANTARCTICA

90°W

South Pole

90°E

Pacific Ocean

70°S

ANTARCTIC CIRCLE

60°S   180°

LARSEN
ICE SHELF

ADELAIDE ISLAND

LAVOISIER ISLAND

RENAUD ISLAND

Grandidier Channel

ARGENTINE ISLANDS

Bismarck Strait

P E N I N S U L A

A N T A R C T I C

Gerlache   Strait

ANVERS
I.

BRABANT I.

PALMER   ARCHIPELAGO

See inset map below

0   1 mile

CORMORANT
I.

HERMIT I.

*Bonaparte
Pt.*

TORGERSEN I.

Palmer Station

*Arthur
Harbor*

LITCHFIELD I.

ANVERS ISLAND

← HUMBLE I.

Bransfield Strait

DECEPTION
ISLAND

SMITH
ISLAND

KING GEORGE
ISLAND

LIVINGSTON
ISLAND

S O U T H   S H E T L A N D   I S L A N D S

SOUTH

GIBBS I.

ELEPHANT
ISLAND

0   50   100

Miles

ANTARCTIC PENINSULA

Bismarck   Strait

See inset map above

Strait

Palmer
Station

JOUBIN
ISLANDS

WIENCKE
ISLAND

*Neumayer
Channel*

× *Mt. Français*

Gerlache

ANVERS ISLAND

*Schollaert
Channel*

MELCHIOR
IS.

BRABANT
ISLAND

0   5   10   20

Miles

gusts of chilling wind. The glaciated peaks then loomed threateningly over the surf-pounded shore, where penguins clustered on the boulders, patiently waiting for whatever it is that only penguins understand.

During the night we ran from Gibbs Island to Stigant Point on the west coast of King George Island, the largest of the South Shetland group. At 5:00 A.M. Bob Dale woke me to report that we were approaching the coast. When I reached the bridge a light granular snow was falling, as it had been all night, the captain told me. In the somber pre-dawn light King George Island was barely visible as a strip of white before which stood black pinnacles, a warning to unwary ships. A strong offshore wind raised quite a chop with whitecaps and streaks of foam. Stretching away to north and south the coastline had a foreboding look—cold and bleak beyond description. Except in a few places where the black pinnacles rose in front of a narrow strip of beach and crumbling rock, remnants of a once great land mass, the icecap terminated in sheer cliffs of blue ice, interrupted here and there by a sloping bank of snow. The ship had been slowed to two or three knots as it edged its way shoreward. Because the west coast of King George Island is thick with submerged columns of rock rising unseen from the bottom like the ones we could see nearer shore, the island has an evil reputation among ship captains and is seldom visited. Stigant Point was thus a refuge for one of the few surviving rookeries of fur seals, the object of our visit. From the ice house we could hear the steady pock, pock, pock of the ship's sonar as it sent signals to right, left, and ahead. The return echoes gave the bearings and distances of the dangerous obstacles so Captain Lenie could safely thread the ship between them.

Clothed in boots and oilskins, two boatloads of us went ashore in Zodiac landing craft, each equipped with a spare outboard motor, surplus gasoline, a tool kit, and two walkie-talkies—all necessary as insurance against unforeseen contingencies in a region where sudden, violent changes in weather are common. This time we made an easy landing on a well-protected cobble beach, and promptly found ourselves in the midst of a chinstrap penguin colony. A short distance away two family groups of fur seals, each consisting of a large bull with his harem of cows and several pups, were stretched out on the beach. During our half day on the island we counted about two hundred fur seals, of which three-fifths were pups. Fur seals have doglike pointed noses, but what sets them off most strikingly from other Antarctic seals is the structure of their hind limbs, which can be folded forward under them to give support for a sitting position and for locomotion on land. The adaptation of the other species of seals has progressed further towards a totally aquatic life; their hind limbs are permanently fixed in a backward direction for use principally in swimming.

The penguins were everywhere: on the shingle beach, on the rock outcrops, and on the snowbanks. The paired birds stood guard on their pebble nests over eggs or downy chicks. The unpaired and bachelor males waddled along in single file or in straggling groups, flippers held out as though for balance. A slope extending from the beach to the top of a ridge more than a hundred feet high was partly covered with dirty, crusted snow, which gave the penguins in a rookery at the top a route along which they were constantly ascending and descending. The broad, pink, webbed feet of the chinstrap species are armed with strong claws that grip the snow. Penguins are indefatigable climbers; despite what appears a clumsy gait and uncertain balance they climb many hundreds of feet over rock and snow in search of ice-free nesting areas. Penguins descending a snowbank often toboggan down it, soiling their white fronts with the dirt left by birds on their way up. Though not afraid of human beings, penguins will make frantic efforts to elude capture and in the process may trip and fall face down, only to go on comically pushing forward with their feet until they regain an upright posture. Awkward and stumbling as penguins are on land, in the water they are the epitome of speed and grace. Before entering the water a penguin will stand poised on a rock, peering out like a hesitant swimmer before an icy plunge; then in an instant it is gone, and you glimpse its speeding body as it disappears into the surf. The return to land is equally dramatic. Abruptly and without warning, a penguin will erupt out of the seemingly untenanted gray water, to land feet first, unerringly as a missile, on the shore. Under water the penguin propels itself with its flipperlike wings, using its feet only for steering.

Venturing around the corner of a cliff, I surprised three immature elephant seals lying in a compact huddle with their heads together. They stared at me out of large, watery, seemingly pupil-less eyes but did not move. Near them three skuas, those gull-like predators that are ubiquitous in the penguin rookeries of the Antarctic, were disputing possession of a penguin carcass. They tugged and pulled at it and threatened one another with raised wings. First one and then another skua would drag the carcass to one side without appreciably increasing its advantage over the others.

At noon we returned to the *Hero*. Our course now followed the coasts of King George Island and of Nelson Island, its neighbor to the south. Seen from the west, the low profiles of these islands appeared quite unlike those of Elephant or Gibbs. Under a cover of snow-white icecaps that broke off precipitously at the coast, they had the even, featureless contour of a convex lens. They appeared to rest on a sea whose tint for several miles offshore was a milky blue, like that of a glacial stream.

The *Hero*'s next destination was the Chilean base on Greenwich Island, a still more southerly member of the South Shetland chain, where we were to embark three Chilean marine biologists. The route to their base took us east through Nelson Strait, a short stretch of water where terrific tide rips can develop. On the afternoon of our passage through the straight the tide was running against the strong east wind, causing a buildup of huge standing waves. Since waves of this kind have a shorter period than sea waves, a small vessel confronting them will be violently tossed about. Ahead of us as we approached the entrance I saw a line of white, which as we drew closer proved to be a band of water in extreme agitation. The largest waves, ten to twelve feet high, were combed everywhere with blowing plumes of spray and streaks of foam. The *Hero*, plunging into this turbulence, rose cleanly over the first wave to drive headlong into the second, lifting masses of water over the bow and hurling spray the full length of the ship. Again and again the ship was tossed up by one wave only to slap down on the next, out of phase at our nine-knot speed with the period between the waves. Sheets of water shot high on either side of the bow, obscuring all view forward. But for all the violence of the tide rip, it was no deterrent to penguins; groups of them swam abeam like porpoises, easily keeping abreast of us as they looped in and out of the waves.

Once we had passed through the tide rip the sea became much calmer. Many miles ahead of us, the white line of the ice-covered Antarctic Peninsula was now clearly visible in the crystalline air. We had entered Bransfield Strait, a broad reach between the South Shetlands and the peninsula that is named for Edward Bransfield, the British claimant to having discovered it in 1820. Turning south, we followed the shores of Robert and Greenwich islands to enter a deep bay in a glacier-locked terrain. From our anchorage off a gravel spit, we could see the Chilean research station, a cluster of orange buildings and radio towers.

With the three biologists aboard, that evening we were on our way to Palmer Station, the American research base on Anvers Island. By the time we sailed it was already growing dark. During the short night we ran through Bransfield Strait and then into Gerlache Strait, a northeast-to-southwest passage between the peninsula and the Palmer Archipelago, and thence into Neumayer Passage, the narrow channel separating Anvers from Wiencke Island. Daylight had returned before we entered Neumayer, where we could now observe how different the conditions in confined waters were from those of more open waters. The approach was dotted

CHINSTRAP PENGUIN (*Pygoscelis antarctica*) COLONY (WITH LONE MACARONI PENGUIN [*Eudyptes chrysolophus*] IN CENTER), STIGANT POINT, KING GEORGE ISLAND

Wherever the rock slopes are bare, chinstraps have taken possession—so completely that it is sometimes difficult to walk between the nests.

CHINSTRAP PENGUINS (*Pygoscelis antarctica*), COUVERVILLE ISLAND

GENTOO PENGUINS (*Pygoscelis papua*), COUVERVILLE ISLAND

ICEBERG, NEAR COUVERVILLE ISLAND

BLUE-EYED CORMORANTS (*Phalacrocorax atriceps*), JOUBIN ISLANDS

BLUE-EYED CORMORANTS (*Phalacrocorax atriceps*), CORMORANT ISLAND

ARCH ICEBERG, BONAPARTE POINT, PALMER STATION

One of the earliest explorers to gather data on formations like this one was Admiral Jules Sebastien César Dumont d'Urville, who on January 22, 1841, claimed this region in the name of France, giving it the name Terre Adélie in honor of his wife. The Adélie penguin is also named after her.

LICHENS, CORMORANT ISLAND

GIANT FULMARS (*Macronectes giganteus*)—LIGHT PHASE, LITCHFIELD ISLAND

GIANT FULMARS (*Macronectes giganteus*)—DARK PHASE, LITCHFIELD ISLAND

DECEPTION ISLAND

This gigantic seal (Mirounga leonina) *weighs up to 9,000 pounds. A rich source of oil, it was nearly extirpated in the last century. Seventeen years of protection prior to World War II permitted the elephant seal to repopulate most of its southern range.*

ELEPHANT SEAL, LITCHFIELD ISLAND

SKUAS (*Catharaeta lonnbergi*), LITCHFIELD ISLAND

Skuas, sometimes called the hawks of the Antarctic, are the only predatory birds of the southern continent. They are extremely aggressive and have been known to knock down a man who inadvertently approached their young too closely.

FIN WHALES (*Balaenoptera physali*), GERLACHE STRAIT

The most abundant of the large whales, the fin whale reaches a maximum length of 85 feet and a weight of 95 metric tons. Whales have been hunted since prehistoric times, as stone-age harpoonheads dating back to 3000 B.C. bear witness. During the Middle Ages, whaling was a monopoly of the Basques, who developed the technique of lancing and roping whales that was followed for centuries. The pursuit of whales in the southern oceans began towards the end of the eighteenth century. With the invention in 1868 of the harpoon gun, the method still used to kill whales, the Antarctic fin whale population has been reduced from 400,000 to about 90,000.

CRABEATER SEAL (*Lobodon carcinophaga*), PALMER STATION

Seals mate under water but give birth and suckle their young on land or ice.

with flat white islands of sea ice; towering here and there among them were sculptured masses of blue ice, small icebergs calved from glaciers on Wiencke and on Anvers Island. We seemed to be entering the mouth of a fjord or a great river debouching from a mountain chasm. Ahead, the walls gradually closed in and the confining mountains rose higher and more steeply; the ice became thicker and the cakes larger, providing basking platforms for seals. Those of the gregarious Weddell species would raise their heads from slumber to stare with a benign curiosity as we passed close by; or, in alarm at the sudden onset of the ship's dark hulk, they would hunch at the edge of the ice raft and plunge over the side. The solitary leopard seals rarely paid us attention; the occasional one that did would simply lift its over-large round head with an air of disdain.

The atmosphere is so clear in Antarctica that one is easily deceived by distances; mountains that seem no more than fifty miles away may in fact be two hundred. And in the absence of haze the colors of distant objects are not like those in other parts of the world. In Antarctica mountains seen at a distance appear yellow rather than blue. Away to the east, as we entered the Gerlache Strait, I saw behind the jagged, lavender-tinted profile of the coastal mountains, the curving surface of the icefield, an expanse of yellow and salmon pink; and far to the south, beyond the end the strait, rose the peninsula's distant yellow peaks, wonderfully distinct even though they were in fact a hundred miles away. At times when our view of the foreground was darkened or cut off by cloud and mist, the peaks farthest away were still visible in the bright sunlight that illuminated them, suggesting to me, as we passed the narrower reaches of the strait, a secret gateway to some elysian region. The farther we pushed into the strait, the more it became crowded with ice and icebergs—almost as though the inanimate forces of nature had resolved to guard the passage against our intrusion.

We passed close to large icebergs which had been wrought into fantastic shapes by the pounding waves and the melting heat of the sun. Below the waterline green grottoes offered a glimpse into dim recesses beyond the reach of day—passages leading downward to the very heart of the iceberg. Above the water, the vertical surfaces of the ice had been worked by wind and sun into honeycomb patterns, flutings, and sculptured fins, or into grotesque shapes suggesting mythological creatures. Except on its highlighted surfaces—or on those where snow had lodged, whose white had a pinkish cast—the iceberg was suffused with a blue tint, which in all recesses, pockets, and grooves deepened to the pure cobalt of a della Robbia medallion, an intense distillation of the ocean's purple hue.

In the narrowest part of Neumayer Passage, where the mountains came down precipitously on either side, the ice became so thick that from a distance it appeared a solid mass from shore to shore. The Hero's speed was now greatly reduced, as Captain Lenie, steering her from the ice house, sought out rifts and channels in the pack. Then, abruptly, the ice came to an end—a sharp line beyond which there was only a scattering of sea-ice cakes and small bergs. As seals began appearing in large numbers on the floes in open water, the captain piloted the ship close enough for the photographers aboard to take pictures. We were now only a few miles from the American base on Anvers Island, which rose on our right, culminating in a series of jagged snow-covered peaks several thousand feet high. Pulling out of the narrow confines of Neumayer Passage into more open water, we moved toward Bismarck Strait on the island's southwestern side. Here Arthur Harbor, an embayment formed by several smaller islands, gives shelter to a jutting formation of ice-free granite that projects from under the great Anvers Island glacier. It is on one side of this formation, which consists of two peninsulas divided by a deep-water inlet, that the Palmer research station is built, the inlet serving as an inner harbor for the station.

As we approached Arthur Harbor, our first sight was of the unoccupied peninsula, which so completely concealed the other from view that my initial glimpse of the station, less than half a mile away, as we rounded a point, came as a considerable surprise. Behind the station the ice field of Anvers Island loomed up, a minatory presence that seemed to declare its implacable intention to wipe this insolent blot from the Antarctic landscape. And off to the left, where the glacier intruded into Arthur Harbor, a fissured precipice which every now and then spewed a massive blue chunk from within its frozen fastness, to send waves racing towards the peninsula, as a further warning—if one were needed—not to misjudge the forces at its command.

When the *Hero* tied up at 9:30 P.M., in broad daylight, on January 13, less than a month had passed since the austral midsummer. On this first visit since leaving Palmer for the winter ten months before, she had arrived over a month behind schedule. Most of the thirty-odd men (there are women at Palmer now, though there were none when I was there) lived in the two main steel and concrete buildings. The station's isolation in winter is so extreme that two buildings, each one completely equipped, had been constructed, so that in the event of fire in one building, a second would be ready to accommodate everyone.

All thirty men at the station turned out to give us a lively welcome, and plans were quickly laid for the four days during which the *Hero* was to remain based at the station. I went to bed late that night, my mind bursting with prospects for the days to come.

On the following day the *Hero* took a party to Port Lockroy, a small island in the entrance to Neumayer Passage that was little more than a gray mound of granite. Around it a curving wall of ice—the front of the glacier that covers much of Wiencke Island—extended for 180 degrees, thus affording considerable protection from the wind. At one time the glacier must have covered the island entirely, but it had retreated long ago. Here in the early years of the century whalers had established a processing plant to which whales killed in the nearby waters were towed for rendering into oil. Little remains of the station today but the bleached whale-bones, lying heaped on a boulder beach at the head of a small cove where the carcasses had been dragged ashore. Curved rib bones lay in jackstraw piles where they had been carelessly discarded. Scattered among them, the huge cylindrical winged segments of the creatures' spines lay in disorder—eloquent testimony to the carnage that took place generations ago.

Much of the rest of the island was occupied by a rookery of gentoo penguins, whose abbreviated white bonnets suggested that they were all female. On pebble nests among the granite ridges, they dozed above their broods of downy gray chicks, most of which were too large to be completely covered. The adults roused from their somnolent state only when joined by their mates or when there was a major disturbance in the rookery.

On the next day there was an excursion to Litchfield Island, noted for the mosses that grow there and also for its nesting skuas and giant petrels. Two Zodiacs were needed to accommodate everyone who wanted to go. Among the group were a University of Minnesota ornithologist, Dr. David Parmelee, and Dr. David Murrish, a physiologist working on penguin circulation, who generously spent his time showing me around.

Litchfield is noted more for its vegetation than for its animal life. The gray granite of its rocky terrain is fissured by a series of steep, narrow clefts or miniature valleys, carpeted with brilliant green and yellow mosses that grow in spongy hummocks dense enough to walk on. Even on the ridges themselves, where the slope was relatively gradual, the mossy growth could reach a depth of eight inches. Small tarns filled the lowest spots in some of the valleys with a brown infusion of thin peaty soil. In just one of these tarns we found an odd, colorless, shrimplike crustacean not more than half an inch long. Bright yellow and orange lichens spotted the granite cliffs in widely separated places; and tufts of a short-bladed grass grew on the exposed tops of some ridges, in pockets of scant soil that had been fertilized by bird droppings and by the dead remains of limpets which gulls had deposited there by the thousands.

The bird population of Litchfield was sparse as compared with some of the smaller islands. In one corner was a small colony of Adélie penguins; and on the opposite side the nests of giant petrels, which are larger than gulls, were distributed by the score over several acres of a rocky headland. The plumage of these birds can vary from brown to almost pure white, with every permutation in between, such as birds with pale heads and brown bodies. Although they did not leave their nests as we approached, they rotated so as always to be facing the intruder and would lunge at anyone who came too close. A blow from one of those large bills would not have caused injury, but there was the risk of being fouled by an oily, malodorous regurgitant. The giant petrels did not offer much resistance to our picking them up to see whether their nests contained eggs or chicks— which would be quickly tucked back into the brood pocket as soon as we released the adult.

The numerous skuas that also nested on Litchfield did not form colonies, but were to be found incubating eggs or protecting young in solitary nests on the stony ground near shore or in the mossy valleys of the interior. They fiercely defended their young with loud, piercing cries and persistent aerial attacks. Divebombing by skuas, heavy birds that attack with fearless determination, is not to be taken lightly. More than one unwary individual has been knocked down by a blow on the head from an angry skua.

Elephant seals are also found on Litchfield Island. Near the bouldery beach where we landed, a herd of a dozen or more elephant seals of both sexes were lying in a compact mass, their brown, loaf-shaped bodies jumbled together so inextricably that it was hard to sort out all their various anatomical parts. On first being disturbed, one head reared up to stare, mouth open wide to show a pink gullet and spiky discolored teeth, then exhaled with a grating rasp, and flopped down again with a groan. This was as much response as we got from these indolent behemoths, lying placidly in their own excrement, until we came close. But then they erupted into a seething mass whose parts began to untangle and disperse, all the while roaring in protest. Some of the animals hurried off into the water; others merely crawled a few yards off and subsided into their former lethargy.

The seals were not confined to the shore but had been able, though with what must have been great effort, to hunch and wriggle themselves deep into some of the valleys, possibly in search of shelter from the wind. In spite of their apparent clumsiness they could travel far and negotiate the considerable heights of that rough terrain. Whatever they had been pursuing—and this remained a mystery—the quest had been disastrous for one elephant seal, whose body we discovered high on one of the ridges: he had crawled or fallen into a deep crack just wide enough to accommodate his body, become wedged there, and perished.

In the protected area of the moss valleys I began to notice while I took photographs that the ground was strewn with what looked like undeveloped feather quills about two inches long, in such quantities that I was puzzled until David Murrish explained that they were molted penguin feathers. During the molting season, when their body insulation is greatly reduced, penguins stay out of the water, gathering in sheltered places where they huddle together to conserve warmth while their new feathers develop. During this time they are unable to eat, since they feed entirely on marine life, but the change is a rapid one, and the renewal of their feathers is completed all at once. Except for ducks, almost all other species of birds molt gradually and thus are able to carry on their normal activities.

On the excursion planned for the next day, we were to go in the *Hero* to the Joubin Islands, which lie fourteen miles west of the station and are the last land barrier protecting Arthur Harbor from the great ocean waves. Beyond them, the empty South Pacific extends for more than six thousand miles, all the way to New Zealand. The Joubins consist of twenty or more low, rocky, tightly clustered islets, some of them separated by the narrowest of channels. The sloping glaciated contours of the islands indicate that at one time they too were covered by the Anvers Island ice cap, and although they are ice-free today, snowbanks fill the sheltered small valleys. The waters around them were uncharted; I was told that no one from the station had yet visited them, and that very possibly no men had ever set foot there. Of course everyone wanted to go, and about fifteen members of the station's scientific staff joined the expedition.

The *Hero* circled the Joubins for an approach from the northwest, feeling her way along by sonar, and came to a stop about a mile from a group of small islands. One rose into a steeply pointed knob, considerably higher than the others. From our position the top of this landmark appeared lighter in color than the surrounding rock, suggesting that a colony of birds might have whitened it with their guano. Among the several landing parties that had been arranged, I chose to go with the ornithologists, among them David Parmelee and Frank Todd, who were looking for Antarctic tern and skua nesting places, and to whom the small pointed island had looked promising. Dr. George Llano, the National Science Foundation's chief polar scientist, went with us. As we approached the island we saw that the top was in fact covered with black-and-white birds. Thinking at first that they were penguins, we soon identified them as blue-eyed shags, the cormorants of the Antarctic. We also could see many white birds circling the top of the island like a pale swarm of gnats; these, Parmelee said, were Antarctic terns. The side of the island we were approaching rose perpendicularly from the water; unable to land here, we followed the shore around to the left and came to a little cove, so narrow that it was hardly more than a slot, in a ragged shelf of rock that jutted out for a distance of two or three hundred feet from the base of the central hill. Some protection from the surf was given here, by rocks that partly blocked the entrance to the slot, and between waves we scrambled out onto the shelf without great difficulty. On shore we found ourselves in the midst of a diving attack by several dozen screaming Antarctic terns. Part of the rocky shelf was bare of snow, but we found no nests with eggs and no young terns. From their aggressive behavior we concluded that the birds must be nesting higher on the island, not far away.

Near our landing place we saw two sheathbills foraging for marine animals among the algae on the rocks that had been exposed by the receding tide. Had it not been for their thick, pale beaks and their Antarctic habitat, one might have mistaken them for white chickens. They not only fed on the shore but also scavenged the refuse around the nests in penguin and cormorant rookeries, where they were accepted with indifference.

Taking my camera and tripod, I began the climb to the top of the island for a look at the cormorant colony. Although the way led up a nearly vertical cliff, of a hard serpentinelike formation, it offered sufficiently secure handholds that, with a companion to hand my equipment up to, I was able to ascend without difficulty. As I crawled over the rim of the cliff I came face to face with a blue-eyed shag on guard at its nest. The bird gawked and jabbed at me but did not fly off; having had little experience with humans, like most other Antarctic birds and animals, these shags were unafraid.

The top of the island was divided by a shallow notch into two peaks, the higher of which—the one I had climbed—was the one occupied by the cormorants. In an area of perhaps two acres, between seventy-five and a hundred pairs of birds were nesting. Most of the nests were circular mounds of mud and pebbles, built up to a height of a few inches and topped by a saucerlike depression in which from two to four taupe-colored downy young birds of various ages were huddled. I saw no nests with eggs, although a few unhatched clutches might possibly have been found by investigating every sitting bird. On every occupied nest, at least one adult was brooding its young or was perched beside them; young birds were never left unguarded. At a few nests both parents were present, one having just returned from a foraging expedition and the other about to take its turn. The young cormorants showed great interest in the recently arrived parent, persistently begging to be fed in a series of tremulous, wavering jabs at its bill. When eventually the adult gave in to the importunities of its off-spring, the young bird fed by plunging its head into the open throat of the parent and receiving food brought up in a series of peristaltic contractions by the adult's esophagus.

When I approached a shag on its nest with deliberation, it would usually remain calm and unperturbed, but at any sudden movement that could be interpreted as a threat, the bird reacted defensively, spreading its wings over its young, umbrella fashion, and facing me with neck outstretched in an attitude of threat. I always retreated when this happened, never testing the courage and fighting spirit of the cormorant by trying to pick up one of its offspring. In this I was motivated as much by the intimidating attitude and formidable size of the shag's bill as by respect for the bird's feelings. These cormorants were strikingly handsome birds, with black and white plumage, red feet, and two fleshy orange caruncles between the eyes and bill. The name of the blue-eyed shag refers not to the color of the iris, which is actually dark brown, but to circles of cobalt blue skin that surround the eyes, giving the birds a goggly, made-up appearance. From chin to legs the entire underplumage is snowy white, and there are also white bars on the wings, most conspicuous during flight, as well as a large rectangular white patch in the middle of the back. The lower back and rump are a dark steely blue, and the rest of the plumage on head, neck, shoulders, wings, and tail is black. The secondary wing feathers, as with some of the northern hemisphere cormorants and other black birds, have a glossy metallic green iridescence.

I remained for some time among the cormorants, photographing them and watching what went on at the nests—the coming and going of the adults to and from their fishing grounds. Often without warning a bird would swoop up over the edge of the cliff and land by a nest almost at my feet. There was an immediate exchange of greetings, with much gawking and neck-stretching as the newcomer waddled up to its mate.

Meanwhile David Parmelee had discovered where the Antarctic tern colony was—on a shoulder of the highest peak of the island, opposite the side I had climbed. Dr. Llano and I were the last two to leave the shag rookery, working our way down to the tern colony by a hazardous route across a snowbank that concealed a sheet of ice. An incautious step here could have resulted in a tumble down a fifty-foot icy slope. But we negotiated the treacherous descent without mishap, arriving at a rocky but more nearly level ridge where the terns screamed all about us.

The nests of most kinds of terns are minimal—generally a few sticks or bits of vegetation laid in a circle around a shallow depression in the ground made by the bird. Antarctic terns make do with even less, merely selecting a slightly concave spot in which to lay their eggs. They are so unfastidious that it does not need even to be on bare ground, but is often strewn with pebbles or shells. On this ridge where the terns nested, pockets in the rocks were filled with limpet shells of remarkably uniform size, each about an inch in diameter. Flat cones shaped like a Chinese peasant's hat, these Antarctic limpets were rough and brown on top, pearly gray-blue inside. What birds had been responsible for dropping the shells on the ridge was a mystery; I suspected skuas, although there were none on the island. Limpets live in the littoral zone, where they hold firmly to the rocks by means of suction when exposed to air at low tide. They are difficult to pry loose then, and although I doubted whether a gull or tern could pry them off, either, I thought a skua might. The great quantity of shells suggested that they were gathered at certain times of the year as a major food resource. In support of my surmise, I had seen such accumulations on Litchfield Island, where many skuas were nesting. I later learned that gulls were responsible.

The most attractive of the Antarctic terns' nests were those placed among the limpets. Without even bothering to rearrange them, the terns had deposited their eggs, usually in clutches of two, on the shells, accepting these fortuitous accumulations as if they had been specifically provided for their convenience. They apparently found the pockets of shells more agreeable than the available stony sites. The terns nesting among limpet shells reminded me of the common terns on the coast of Maine, which lay eggs among blue mussel shells deposited above the tide line by crows and gulls. In Antarctica the contrast between eggs and background was subtler, the dark, spotted, olive-brown eggs blending more completely with the brown and gray-blue shells around them.

On this small peak, in such limited space as was not occupied by the blue-eyed shags, Parmelee estimated that there were a hundred Antarctic tern nests. Among the adults, swooping to attack, protesting our intrusion with vociferous staccato cries—*keree keree*—were many juveniles, recognizable by their white heads. If these immature birds had been hatched that year, then either the eggs we found had been laid by very late breeders or else, more probably, they were second attempts at nesting by birds that had lost first a brood of eggs or young to predators.

Before returning to the *Hero* we visited two other islands. The first, much larger than the cormorant island, was a low, gray dome of rock devoid of vegetation except for a firm blackish variety of moss occurring in protected places and a luxuriant growth of snow algae in a snowbank at the head of the cove where we landed. Depressions in the snow were given a rather dingy or sooty appearance by the algae, whose green was not particularly noticeable until closely examined. Wherever we broke the surface by walking on it, however, bright green pockets of algae would be exposed. Not all snow algae are green; some forms are red and others yellow, adding their own distinctive tint to extensive snowfields on the mountains of the Antarctic Peninsula.

When we reached the snowbank, a group of six or eight Weddell seals were sprawled sleeping in the sun. They ignored us until we had approached to within a few feet; then they raised their heads and stared only to sink back with a sigh—except for one seal, more agitated than the others, that lumbered and wriggled down to the water and swam off.

A large flock of skuas used the highest point of the island as a roost, and they circled overhead as we landed. We found no nests. On the opposite side of the cove from where we had disembarked, many Dominican gulls were standing about; but they too were using the island only as a resting place. Since the island had turned out to be the next thing to a biological desert, we now chose a small one where we had seen a colony of penguins.

This colony turned out to be of especial interest to the ornithologists because not only were all three species—Adélies, gentoos, and chinstraps—represented, but also, although the majority occupied separate areas according to their kind, in some small groups they were mixed together, gentoos nesting beside chinstraps and chinstraps beside Adélies, or with all three in one group, contrary to the accepted belief that penguins maintain a strict segregation by species. David Parmelee was excited because just such a mixing of species had not been observed before, although in some chinstrap penguin colonies in the South Shetland archipelago a few macaroni penguins, breeding south of their normal range, have been recorded. However, mixed colonies of birds in other parts of the world are quite common; thus snowy egrets, Louisiana herons, and little blue herons frequently intermingle in rookeries, and herring gulls and great black-backed gulls share the same small islands off the coast of Maine. Because of the great importance they attached to their discovery, David Parmelee and Frank Todd made a count of the penguins in this mixed colony. The count of the three penguin species in this Joubin Island colony was published in the Antarctic Journal of the United States.

CHINSTRAPS	GENTOOS	ADÉLIES
37 nests, 72 birds	59 nests, 118 birds	100± pairs
3 with eggs	4 with eggs	eggs and chicks not counted
9 with one chick	14 with one chick	
22 with two chicks	38 with two chicks	
2 with three chicks	3 with one chick and one egg	

While the count was in progress, a chinstrap trying to return to its nest passed through a nesting group of gentoos, which displayed great hostility to its encroachment. The chinstrap, making itself as tall and thin as possible, ran the gauntlet, dodging from side to side to avoid the jabbing beaks, uttering a despairing croak when a blow struck home, but never retaliating.

Cormorant Island is situated five miles east of Palmer Station, a short distance from the glacial front on Anvers Island. It is ice-free, a medium-sized island with very rough terrain consisting of broken ridges of naked rock running parallel with the Anvers shore. In many ways Cormorant Island resembles Litchfield. It was named for its colony of cormorants, the nearest such colony to the station. This year, possibly because of depredations by skuas, by late in the season nearly every shag had lost its eggs or young and had been unable to lay another clutch. The nests we found were those few that had survived the predation and a small number of second tries.

On the fourth day that we were based at Palmer, we went to Cormorant Island, making the trip in two Zodiacs which got us there in a little less than an hour. The day was cloudless except for streaks of high cirrus; a moderate wind blew, and the temperature was in the forties—a warm day for Antarctica. We threaded our way through hundreds of small ice cakes, sloughings from the Anvers Island glacier, which speckled the ultramarine-dark sea. To me the journey was like many a summer boat trip I had taken, and indeed that is exactly what it was—an austral summer boat ride. The wind was astern and the air was so extremely dry that I felt no cold.

We landed on a smooth, sloping ledge, an easier and a safer place to disembark than a cobble beach, and hauled the Zodiac out high and dry. The landing place was on the side of a headland of fractured and angular rocks, separated by a boulder beach from a lower but equally cloven and jumbled hill. When all the gear had been unloaded, everyone headed for the interior, each with his own particular goal in mind. Taking a route from the beach across a rock-strewn plain that sloped gently up to the middle of the island, I was able to place my cameras so as to obtain a good general view of the island.

My first impression was one of grayness and sharp unweathered edges, of recently broken and shifted blocks of stone. From where I stood the land sloped straight down towards the rugged and more exposed shore of the island and towards Bismarck Strait. As I looked around, trying to decide where to go next, a pair of skuas dived at me; I had to hold my tripod over my head to keep from being struck. Uttering fierce cries, they came at me fast and low, and with such obvious determination that I ducked involuntarily despite my tripod shield. Then, seeing two young skuas nearby, I moved hurriedly away.

From where I stood the view to the northeast was spectacular almost beyond belief. Here and there in the foreground, along the shore of Cormorant Island with its jagged heaps of rock, groups of Adélie penguins stood beside their nests. A strip of blue sea lay between the shore and the perpendicular edge of the Anvers

Island glacier, whose smooth white upper surface curved away towards the horizon; and rising behind this great expanse into a sky filmy with clouds, towered a range of shining pyramidal mountains. Near at hand, the gray monotony of the rocks was broken by splashes of orange and yellow lichens. Some rock faces were so completely covered, whereas others in similar situations were bare of them, that I wondered what the controlling factors were. In a temperate climate, on mountain tops below five thousand feet, lichens would have covered every available surface, their colors varying from green through black, gray, and white, but with not much orange except near the sea. Although it was my first impression that lichens here in the Antarctic were mostly of one brightly pigmented kind, this was not borne out by careful inspection; just as in other parts of the world, if any at all are found, innumerable varieties are present.

Following the disastrous reduction of the cormorants by predation, the most numerous birds on the island were now the Adélie penguins. Gentoos and chinstraps may have been present in smaller colonies, but I did not look for them. The other breeding birds were skuas, giant petrels, and Wilson's storm petrels. David Parmelee found a few Wilson's storm petrels nesting deep in narrow crevices and under projecting rocks, places inaccessible to the prying skuas.

III. MISFORTUNE AT DECEPTION ISLAND

On January 18, at 9:00 A.M., the *Hero* left Palmer Station on a northbound cruise for Deception Island, the southernmost of the South Shetland group. Her first call was at Domer Island to pick up Larry Schock, who was looking for an opportunity to photograph seals. The voyage through Neumayer Passage was made during the middle of the day, when the conditions of light and atmosphere were less spectacular than on the voyage south. We passed many crabeater, leopard, and Weddell seals, lolling on the flat rafts of sea ice, indifferent to our approach.

The weather was holding beautifully calm when we entered Bransfield Strait and Captain Lenie agreed to divert the ship to Couverville Island so that Frank Todd could look for the snow petrels reported to be breeding there. Couverville lies on the east side of Bransfield Strait, in a bay close to the Antarctic Peninsula shore, where it is well protected from bad weather. It is a fairly large island, consisting of a thousand-foot mountain with a wide shelf extending out from its steep western slope. On its north side the mountain drops precipitously into the bay; here in cracks and on ledges Dominican gulls were nesting. On a buttress of rock at the foot of the cliff, blue-eyed shags had established a small colony. The most accessible part of the island, and the place where Frank Todd and I went ashore, was the low western extension, where several groups of gentoo and chinstrap penguins in separate rookeries were established on rocky knolls near the water. We found no snow petrels, but the setting of the island and the fortunate conditions at the time of our visit made it a memorable one.

Looking west from our side of Couverville, we saw a medium-sized bay ringed with a sawtooth of snow-covered peaks capped with cottony white clouds. In the bay floated many icebergs, including a few very large ones, intricately sculptured by wind and sun. The wind had ceased to blow and the glassy surface of the bay, barely disturbed by parallel ripples, reflected in alternate bands the warm afternoon light and the crystalline blue of the sky. Dark against this background, the penguins stood by their nests on the bleak gray foreground shore. Mosher came to pick us up far from where we had been landed, and we motored back to the *Hero* through a bizarre world for which man is ill-fitted and which he should penetrate with caution.

That evening in Bransfield Strait Captain Lenie sighted a small pod of fin whales swimming and spouting on the surface. They were feeding on a large school of krill whose presence was fuzzily reflected on the ship's sonar. We sailed into the midst of the whales without seeming to disturb them and saw the wisps of condensed moisture from their lungs whenever one of them blew. A few times a whale sounded near us, and we would see its flukes raised clear of the water as it slid below the surface without a splash.

We came within sight of our destination early on the morning of January 19. Deception Island is of volcanic origin, and must have been several thousand feet higher than at present before its top collapsed in a cataclysmic event that left a great crater or caldera, five miles across, which opens to the sea through a gap less than half a mile wide and thus constitutes an excellent all-weather harbor. During the last century a Norwegian whaling station had been established here; it was finally abandoned at the onset of the Second World War. In 1957–58, during the International Geophysical Year, several nations established research bases within the crater. On the left-hand shore as one enters, Argentina built her station, and the Chileans set up theirs on the opposite side of the lagoon. It is easy to guess that territorial rivalry was the true motivation behind these stations. Although in 1961 the Antarctic Treaty put all disputed claims in abeyance, the unofficial assertion (despite official protestations to the contrary) of national claims on the Antarctic Peninsula and its associated islands still continues.

Near the abandoned whaling station, the British have likewise built a research laboratory. As recently as 1967, an eruption destroyed the Chilean station and so severely damaged the British one, only a few miles away, that it too had to be evacuated. The volcano, whose activity centered on the rim of the caldera behind these bases, had rained hot ash on the Chilean buildings and burned them to the ground; only twisted metal skeletons were left standing. The Chileans had fled along the shore to the British base—which, although not set on fire, was rocked by earthquakes, setting crazily askew the old whaling station's rendering furnaces with their storage tanks and chimneys.

Shortly after six o'clock on that morning, we passed through the entrance to the harbor. As the ship approached this gateway in the light of dawn, towering cliffs rose on either side; on the one hand, black compacted lava and cinders were piled up into a serrated peak, and on the other a massive flat-topped cliff of yellow ocher stood guard over the entrance. Looming behind these ramparts, two thousand feet high, the highest point on the snow-capped rim of the great caldera shone pink in the morning sun. The ocher cliff just inside the entrance gave way to a series of benches. The lowest, at sea level, was composed of maroon cinders gullied by erosion into buttresses shaped like a row of ninepins. Resting on this bottom layer was a steep ocher-colored setback formation above which a more gradual incline, consisting of dark volcanic material, rose toward the white top of the rim several hundred feet above.

While the *Hero* was engaged in collecting bottom samples within the crater, Larry Schock, Frank Todd, and I went ashore in a Zodiac. We landed on the cinder beach in front of the ruined Chilean buildings, where a flow of hot water had formed a steaming pool dammed off from the cold sea in the lagoon. A gentoo penguin, which may have been a sick bird, lay unresponsive on the warm ash beside the pool. On the slope back of the station the outpouring of black frothy cinders and lava had laid down a complex of tumbled ridges from which I saw that vapor was still escaping in places. Climbing the cinder slope, I had a magnificent view of the entire crater lagoon. Off in the middle, I saw the *Hero*, which at that distance, appeared no bigger than a child's toy. Looking in the opposite direction, towards the snow-covered rim of the crater, I could see ample evidence of the eruption that had taken place eight years before. Extending almost to the top of the crater was a jumble of scoriaceous lava, its mounds and ridges set off by depressions and sheer faults which exposed the red, burned-out interior of the flow. High up near the scene of the eruption, Antarctic terns, their white wings flickering in the sun, were circling and alighting. They had chosen this improbable, remote place to colonize.

Returning to the beach, we boarded the Zodiac for a trip of several miles, skirting the shore, for a look at the wreckage of the whaling station. On the way we passed a bluff composed of stratified snow and ash, with the look of banded onyx where pieces of it had fallen off—alternating falls of snow and cinders, over a period of many years, that had been preserved by the insulating properties of the volcanic material. At our destination, companies of chinstrap penguins stood about among the rusting boilers, the tilting stacks, the broken, half-buried machinery, and the beached wooden whaleboats, now weathered to a silvery gray. Near by, at the British research base—where littered rooms, smashed windows, unlatched doors swinging in the wind, the locked hangar still housing its De Havilland airplane, and untapped drums of aviation fuel, spoke of a hurried evacuation—terns greeted us with sharp cries, hovering above us and diving at us halfheartedly. The young had flown but the old birds still claimed possession. The whaling station and the deserted scientific facilities were fast reverting to these earlier inhabitants. The following day, January 20, was one I shall never forget. Early in the morning the *Hero* sailed out of the calm waters of the lagoon and took up a position not far from Deception, alongside a small volcanic island, a core of lava that rose precipitously out of deep water. While divers were collecting marine specimens from the island's underwater shelf, Frank and Larry and I were to be landed at a point on Deception Island itself that was occupied by a large colony of chinstrap penguins. Our purpose was to search for macaroni penguins, which, as I have mentioned, are sometimes found breeding in small numbers among those of other species.

The sea was choppy, and breaking waves sloshed against the shore. As our landing craft approached the eroded cliff, we could see that getting ashore would not be easy. The tide was out, and extending into the sea for a dozen yards was a littoral zone, a wave-sculptured lava bench, each serrated point of which was clothed in slippery dark-green algae. Carlos, the boatman, proposed looking along the coast for a better place than these forbidding rocks, but the consensus was to attempt a landing here. So Carlos ran the Zodiac into a little inlet between lava pinnacles; Frank jumped out, Larry followed on the next wave, and I handed him my camera case. At that moment a big swell raised the Zodiac high against the jagged shore. Grabbing a point of lava with my left hand, I was about to step out when in the backsurge the boat suddenly dropped five feet, leaving me suspended between it and the rock.

My right hand lost its grip and I fell sideways into the water, twisting my left shoulder. For a moment I found myself plunged waist-deep in the frigid Antarctic sea. Then, with Larry's help and much puffing on my part (I remember wondering at the time what all the noise was about, as though it had been someone else who was making it) I scrambled out. Feeling a sharp pain in my left shoulder, I now realized that my left arm was useless.

While Frank, having told Carlos to take me straightaway back to the *Hero*, was sending a radio message on our walkie-talkie, I managed somehow, half rolling and half falling, to get back into the Zodiac as it rose on another wave. Larry, handing back my camera case at my insistence, announced that he too was coming along—a decision that sent a surge of gratitude through me.

We started back at such high speed over the choppy sea that every bump was like a knife stabbing into my shoulder, and I had to ask Carlos to slow down. As we drew near the *Hero* all the crew and the captain were at the rail and the Jacob's ladder had been lowered.

How I was pulled on board I don't remember. But soon Captain Lenie had me below on the mess deck, where Bob Rogers was waiting with a half tumbler of Cutty Sark, which he ordered me to drink. Seldom have I tasted anything so good, and the effect was immediate. Next the captain and the cook undressed me and put me into a hot shower. This is the standard treatment for exposure, given to anyone who falls into sub-freezing Antarctic waters. The limit for survival in water at that temperature is said to be twenty minutes.

My trouble, however, was not so much exposure as it was the injured shoulder. Not much knowledge of anatomy was required to see that it had been dislocated. I told the captain what I remembered from my medical-school days about how to treat a shoulder dislocation. The only trouble was that I didn't remember the whole procedure: that the arm should be rotated as it is pulled. First Captain Lenie tried and failed, as he thought, because he wasn't strong enough. Then Larry, who is about six feet three, had a go at it, but without success. Both the captain and Larry were afraid of hurting me, but in fact the pulling felt good. Now there was nothing to do but seek help elsewhere. The captain went off to the radio shack, and returned to tell me that the British ship *Endurance*—a large vessel that, like American icebreakers, carries two helicopters—was not far away, had been reached by radio, and was sending over the ship's doctor.

Under the influence of the whisky, I had soon fallen asleep. I was awakened two hours later by the presence of the captain, leaning over me to say that the doctor was on board. I was much entertained by all the preparations that ensued—especially when the doctor, a very young Britisher in a parachuter's uniform, began thumbing through an illustrated pamphlet on the treatment of dislocations. After a few manipulations he said the joint was back in place, my arm was bound into a tight sling, and I was put back to bed. When he told me that my arm would have to remain in a sling for six weeks, I knew that all photography for this season in Antarctica was over.

Meanwhile consultations had been going on between the captain and the doctor, and by radio with Bob Dale at Palmer. Deciding that an X-ray photograph should be taken, they got in touch with the Russians at Bellingshausen Station on King George Island, where X-ray equipment was available. The *Hero* proceeded there and arrived at 7:00 P.M. (6:00 P.M. Russian time). I was wrapped up and whisked ashore. I found that I could walk, although my shoulder hurt at every jolt.

The Russian station consisted of three main buildings—a mess hall, administrative offices, and a medical building, all boxlike structures painted in pastel colors. Although they looked flimsy, they must have been well insulated since they were occupied the year around. During the summer, at the time I was there, about forty men lived at the station. Most of them slept in a long, low dormitory set back from the beach and behind the main buildings. Inside, the Russians' quarters had a primitive and temporary appearance as compared to those at Palmer. When the Russian doctors, Mikhail Pozdnev and Vasilii Vozonov, were ready for me, I was led over to the medical building and ushered into a small room which could be called the surgery. In the middle of the surgery stood a strange yellow object with a funnel-shaped tube projecting from one side. This was the X-ray apparatus. Two pictures were taken and immediately developed. They showed a slightly compacted fracture of the head of the humerus (the main upper arm bone) and a splinter off the shaft near the head. The two doctors promptly set about putting my shoulder into a plaster cast. As they did, they murmured volubly in Russian. I had perfect confidence in them.

I was then taken back to the manager's office where arrangements were being made to transfer me by helicopter to the Coast Guard icebreaker *Glacier*. Since the *Glacier* would not be in the vicinity for four or five days, the Russians had agreed to put me up.

The next morning, after breakfast—a strange concoction of cut-up sausage mixed with a sweetish substance that might have been cabbage, and tea (*chai*)—the helicopter from the *Endurance* landed on the beach and I said farewell to the British doctor. One of the Russian doctors, Vasilii Vozonov, asked if I would like to walk to an observation hut on the other side of the island. Since the island at this point was only a kilometer wide, I quickly agreed. We set off across a bulldozed area that was being prepared as a landing strip. My companion said we would see elephants, meaning elephant seals, and would look out over the Drake Passage. We also encountered skuas, which appeared less aggressive than most, with Antarctic terns diving at them. (The Russian name for a tern, *kerechki*, mimics the sound these birds make.) On a cinder beach several cow elephant seals bellowed at us with wide-open mouths. They were molting and looked ragged.

At the far end of the beach near old volcanic cliffs stood a small rectangular hut. Painted on the side were some Russian words and, in English, "The Penguin Observation Post," with the image of a large penguin alongside. Entering through a vestibule, I found myself in a room with bunks on either side, between which a

DANCING ADÉLIE PENGUINS, McMURDO SOUND

ICE CAVE, HUT POINT PENINSULA

This peninsula is the site of the camp established by Captain Robert Falcon Scott on his first expedition to the Antarctic, in 1901–4.

EMPEROR PENGUINS (*Aptenodytes forsteri*), McMURDO SOUND

Captain Frank Worsley, the navigator for Shackleton's 1914–16 expedition, wrote of the killer whale: "Mouth has a four feet stretch—one, after being harpooned and cut up, contained twelve seals and ten porpoises. They will attack [in a pack] a blue whale which may weigh a hundred tons." The largest member of the dolphin family, the killer whale may grow to a length of thirty feet.

KILLER WHALES (*Orcinus orca*), McMURDO SOUND

*Following the molt, which takes place in late Feb-
ruary, Adélie penguins leave their rookeries at Cape
Bird on Ross Island and on Cape Royds—the
southernmost of all penguin rookeries—for the open
water of McMurdo Sound. From there they migrate
north to spend the winter in the pack ice south of the
Antarctic Convergence.*

ADÉLIE PENGUINS (*Pygoscelis adeliae*) AND KILLER WHALE (*Orcinus orca*), McMURDO SOUND

*In the cold dark of the Antarctic winter, eggs are
laid, chicks hatch, and the young are reared. It is
not until October, when the young are nearly full
grown and the ice has begun to break up, that the
colony disperses. Then the unpaired adults travel
northward on the floating ice, to be followed by the
parents with molting chicks. Numbers of these emperor penguins appear in McMurdo Sound, where
during the Antarctic summer they gorge themselves
in preparation for the annual molt. This process,
which imposes a period of fasting, takes place out
on the pack ice of the Ross Sea.*

EMPEROR PENGUINS (*Aptenodytes forsteri*), McMURDO SOUND

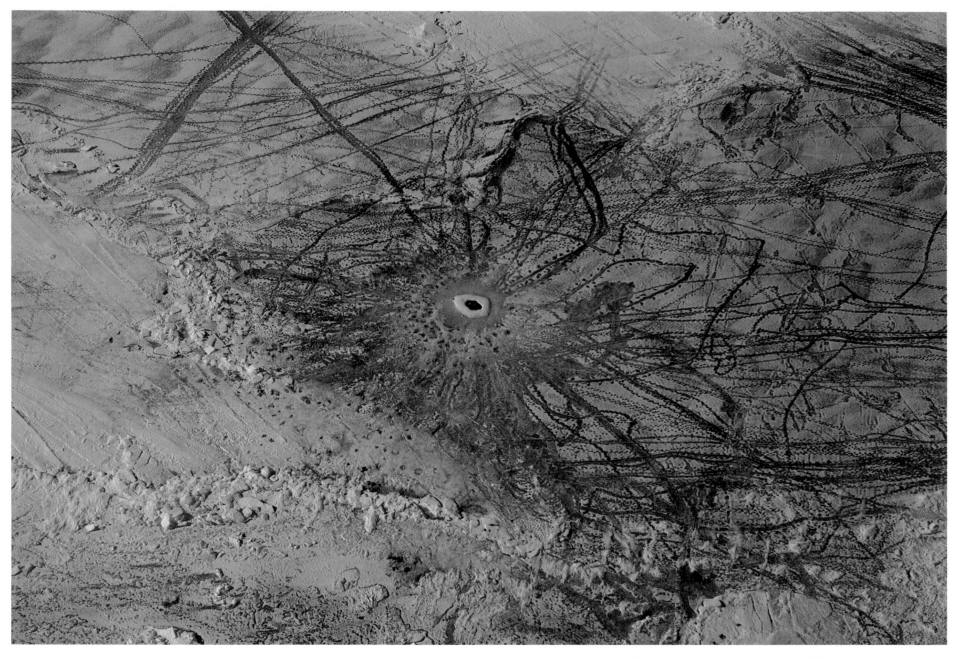

WEDDELL SEAL (*Leptynochtes weddelli*) BREATHING HOLE WITH PENGUIN AND SEAL TRACKS, McMURDO SOUND

The Weddell seal maintains breathing holes in fixed sea ice; in the austral summer, these holes are used also by the Adélie and emperor penguins.

WEDDELL SEALS (*Leptynochtes weddelli*), HUTTON CLIFFS, NEAR HUT POINT PENINSULA

A British seal hunter, James Weddell, gave his name to the sea he first penetrated, in 1823, and to the species of seal shown here. Young seals grow fat on the rich milk of their mothers, adding weight at the rate of five pounds a day from a birth weight of sixty. They are taught to swim and to come to the surface to breathe. While the pups are putting on several hundred pounds, their mothers lose at least as much.

ICE CAVE, HUT POINT PENINSULA

FRESH-WATER POND, DAILEY ISLANDS, McMURDO SOUND

ANCHOR-ICE SPONGE, BLACK ISLAND, SOUTH McMURDO SOUND

VOLCANIC CINDERS AND ICE, DAILEY ISLANDS

KOETTLITZ GLACIER, FROZEN POND—NEAR ROYAL SOCIETY RANGE

Koettlitz Glacier was one of the regions whose geology was explored by members of the Scott expedition of 1910–13 who did not take part in the ill-fated journey to the South Pole. The glacier is named for Dr. Reginald Koettlitz, who was Scott's senior scientist on this expedition.

double glass window looked onto the open sea. There was a kerosene stove at the foot of one of the beds. We sat on the bunks and presently a stamping of feet announced the arrival of two thickset Russians. They were clean-shaven, unlike Vasilii who wore a short cropped beard and mustache. Vasilii introduced us and we shook hands. The conversation, none of which I understood, became animated. Soon more footsteps were heard and a third man entered. He wore a full beard. His face was attractively craggy, his expression kindly and humorous, and he spoke fairly good English. The three were all biologists; the bearded man, Lief Popov, specialized in marine life. The first two had sharply pointed noses which gave an alert expression to their wide Slavic faces.

After some general conversation, in whose bawdy humor I was included thanks to Lief's interpretations, he suggested tea. Having finally succeeded in lighting the kerosene stove, he put on a very black kettle to heat. While we were waiting for the water to boil, one of the biologists dug under the mattress of the bed opposite to the one I was sitting on and produced a bottle containing a clear liquid. He measured the level of the liquid and, indicating a higher level, announced in English, "Fifty-fifty." He went out with the bottle, I presumed to add an equal amount of water, and returned with it nearly full. Then three mugs and a small plastic cup with Japanese lettering were produced; the cup had been found on the beach and was the sort the Japanese use for saki. Into these one of the men poured liberal amounts of the clear concoction, the basic ingredient of which must have been an Argentine brandy, and added a dash of lemon juice from another bottle labeled "Best Seller," which he had taken off a shelf. From the strength of the mixture, I judged that the original liquor must have been nearly straight alcohol. Lief found some crackers to go with the drinks. They were hard as rocks and he laughingly called them Robert Scott biscuits (the expedition during which the explorer died on his way back from the South Pole was in 1912). After three rounds of alcohol I was feeling more relaxed and agreeable than ever. The Russian hosts had drunk much more than I, and were also having a good time.

After two cups of tea each, they suggested a walk along the beach to another cove where there was a herd of elephant seals. We counted twenty-seven of the animals in two groups, that lay massed together.

After returning to the hut, we all walked back to the mess hall at the base for the noon meal. There my incapacity was recognized by everyone, and I received help with whatever seemed to be giving me difficulty, whether it was buttering bread, serving myself from the common pots, cutting food, or scraping my plate when I had finished eating. Even though I became quite adept at managing buttons and the loops on my jacket with one hand, my hosts still insisted on helping me with such things. I found that in the long run it was simpler to surrender to their care. Vasilii—who called me "Mr. Pierker"—even insisted on putting tooth powder on my toothbrush and then on washing my hand. It made me think of the Zen koan, "What is the sound of one hand clapping?"

Vasilii also wrote me laconic notes composed with the help of a Russian-English dictionary. One of these read, "Tomorrow go visit Adélie Colony penguin and not be bored?" With Mikhail, Vasilii's youthful room-mate, communication was more direct, frequently resorting to sign language when he found himself at a loss for the correct English word. Mikhail had a pleasant smile, and I thought I detected a poetic side in his nature when he showed me a picture of his seven-year-old daughter, very plump and Russian-looking in a white fur hat.

Because of having to lie always on my back or slightly on one side and because of the sagging bed, I slept badly. The ache in my left arm was worst at night. To add to the discomfort, my legs also began aching then, and there was a further problem: the toilet in the medical building was not functioning, and since I was sure that the Russians would not approve of one's using the outdoors, answering a call of nature at night meant that I had to get completely dressed and slog through the snow or the mud to the next building. Because of this I did not get undressed until I was ready to sleep, and planned my liquid consumption with care—which called for going to bed thirsty.

After a few days, the novelty of living at a Russian outpost had worn off, and I began to feel bored. There was no place where I could sit comfortably except the manager's office, as I had been invited to do, but where the door was always shut, or in the mess hall where a loudspeaker was always blaring with Russian music or voices declaiming what I took to be revolutionary principles.

So much of the time I sat uncomfortably in the surgery or lay on my bed. On January 21 and 22 I had a walk in the morning and slept in the afternoon. But on January 23 a gale was blowing. With visibility down to half a mile, there would be no walk that day. The British ship *Bransfield* had been scheduled to call but had canceled her visit because of the weather. So the possibility of getting to the Falklands that way, and of flying from Stanley to Buenos Aires, was now out of the question. The next chance of leaving the Russian base would be the *Glacier*, due to arrive on January 25. If the weather kept up that too might be impossible, and then there was no telling when I would get away. I now felt totally cut off from the outside world.

All day the weather got worse. The wind from the east increased and brought snow with it. In Antarctica this was only a summer storm, but at home we would have called it a blizzard. In any event, it was too severe to permit a helicopter to land. The next day it was blowing hard and snowing, but the overcast looked brighter and the barometer had begun to rise. The *Bransfield* and the *Lindblad Explorer* were reported holed up in a good harbor; the *Glacier*'s whereabouts were not known.

This was the day when Vasilii and Mikhail were finally to change my bandages. I had been looking forward to the procedure as something to break the monotony, and hoping for a new cast that would be more comfortable. But they only cut off the old one—revealing a shoulder and chest that were appallingly black and blue—lined it with fresh cotton padding, and put it back on, again, held in place with bandages.

With the *Lindblad Explorer* due the next day at noon, I was hoping that she would be on her way back to Ushuaia so that I could be on my way. And indeed on that day, January 25, the weather was much improved; the wind had dropped and there was no precipitation. After breakfast I heard a helicopter overhead and, as I was going out to investigate, the British doctor from the *Endurance* walked in. As I listened to his conversation with the Russians, it became clear that the *Explorer* was on her way south, so that if I were taken on board I would be returned to Palmer. The position of the *Glacier* was unknown, but she was presumed icebound, perhaps in Arthur Harbor. The Russians thought I should wait for the *Glacier* rather than go on the *Explorer*, which would not be returning to Ushuaia for ten days. I learned also that the *Endurance* had lost one of her survey boats off Nelson Island, where the anchor chain had parted and the boat had been smashed against the rocks. It had taken three days to rescue the party marooned by the wreck, who had also lost their tents in the storm. Likewise because of the storm, the *Endurance* had been unable for three days to carry on any surveying or sounding.

Later that day I learned that the *Glacier* was due on January 28—three days more! The sky cleared and the sun came out. There was no wind. I went for a walk with Vasalii. Later, shortly before supper, Mikhail asked me if I would like him to read a poem in Russian. He read Pushkin's poem on Peter I, reciting a good deal of it from memory. He read well as far as I could judge, with much expression but not overdramatically.

The snow that had fallen during the two-day storm was rapidly melting, and the base quickly became an island of mud. The clothes I had been wearing—consisting entirely of those issued by the N.S.F.—were getting dirty, and I had nothing else with me—no clean underwear, no clean socks or handkerchief, one soiled cotton shirt, boots and sneakers but no shoes, and no way to launder anything. What I would have liked more than anything was a bath. That was impossible because the Russians had no running water, hot or cold, no shower, and no place I ever saw for doing one's own laundry. Even brushing one's teeth was difficult. Each of the three main buildings had one washbasin with a small tank above it. At the bottom of the tank was a valve connected to a rod which hung down. You got water by joggling the rod; with skill you could wet your toothbrush but it was hard to rinse your mouth because the tank was too low to put your head under. It appeared that I would arrive in Albuquerque—I hoped before too much longer—wearing soiled red socks and sneakers, a soiled flannel shirt, soiled longjohns, soiled khaki pants, with oily hair and a runny nose.

Later the next day, word came that the *Glacier* would arrive tomorrow. When I went out for breakfast on the following morning I saw in the harbor a large red ship that turned out to be the *Lindblad Explorer*. Soon tourists in orange parkas and waterproof trousers began landing from the ship's small boats and crowding into the office of the assistant manager, where various Russian souvenirs had been laid out for sale. It seemed to me a comical and incongruous sight: fashionable women in oilskins—the younger ones much made up under their waterproof hoods—buying those cheaply made fur hats. The tourists did not stay long; within an hour and a half they had re-embarked, and I went back to my bed in the surgery to read and wait for the *Glacier* to arrive. After a short while I heard the sound of a helicopter, and after quickly putting the last items into my suitcase I went outside. From then on everything happened fast. At the door was Vasilii, excitedly announcing, "American helicopter." A Sikorski HH-52, a medium-sized craft, was settling into a landing near the beach.

By the time I had carried my bags one by one out of the manager's office building, the helicopter had landed, and a Russian was hastily raising the American and Russian flags over the office building. Noticing that the American flag was upside down, I drew a picture on a plank to explain the error, which he quickly corrected. Whether the co-pilot, who had jumped out of the helicopter and was taking a picture of the building, had recorded the gaffe, I did not find out.

Advancing toward the helicopter, I was greeted by an American in an aviator's suit, who invited me to get on board. He was one of three members of a team that had come from the *Glacier* to inspect the base as provided for in the Antarctic Treaty. My baggage was in many willing Russian hands, and most of the Russians I had gotten to know in the last week came up to say goodbye. I was strapped into a seat opposite the door, the engine accelerated, and without a quiver the machine very slowly lifted itself off the gravel and began moving out over the bay. The *Glacier*, anchored in another cove, was not in sight. After a stop on a beach to pick up three whalebones which almost filled the helicopter, we flew on for a landing on the *Glacier*'s flight deck that was just as gentle as the takeoff had been.

That night, after a shower and a change into clean clothes—with the cast removed and my arm in a sling—I dined in the wardroom with the ship's officers and with Frank Todd and David Parmelee, who were also on their way back to the United States. I greatly enjoyed this return to civilized amenities, and slept well that night in my American-designed berth.

By early afternoon the next day, after an inspection of the Chilean station, we were steaming north towards South America. The crossing of the Drake Passage was smoother than might have been expected, and on January 30 the *Glacier* was standing by at the eastern entrance to the Beagle Channel to await the Argentine pilot. By around nine that evening I was in Miami, where I stayed in the airport hotel. The next morning I flew west to Houston, Dallas, and finally Albuquerque. The date was February 3, it was winter in New Mexico, and I was happy to be home again for a while.

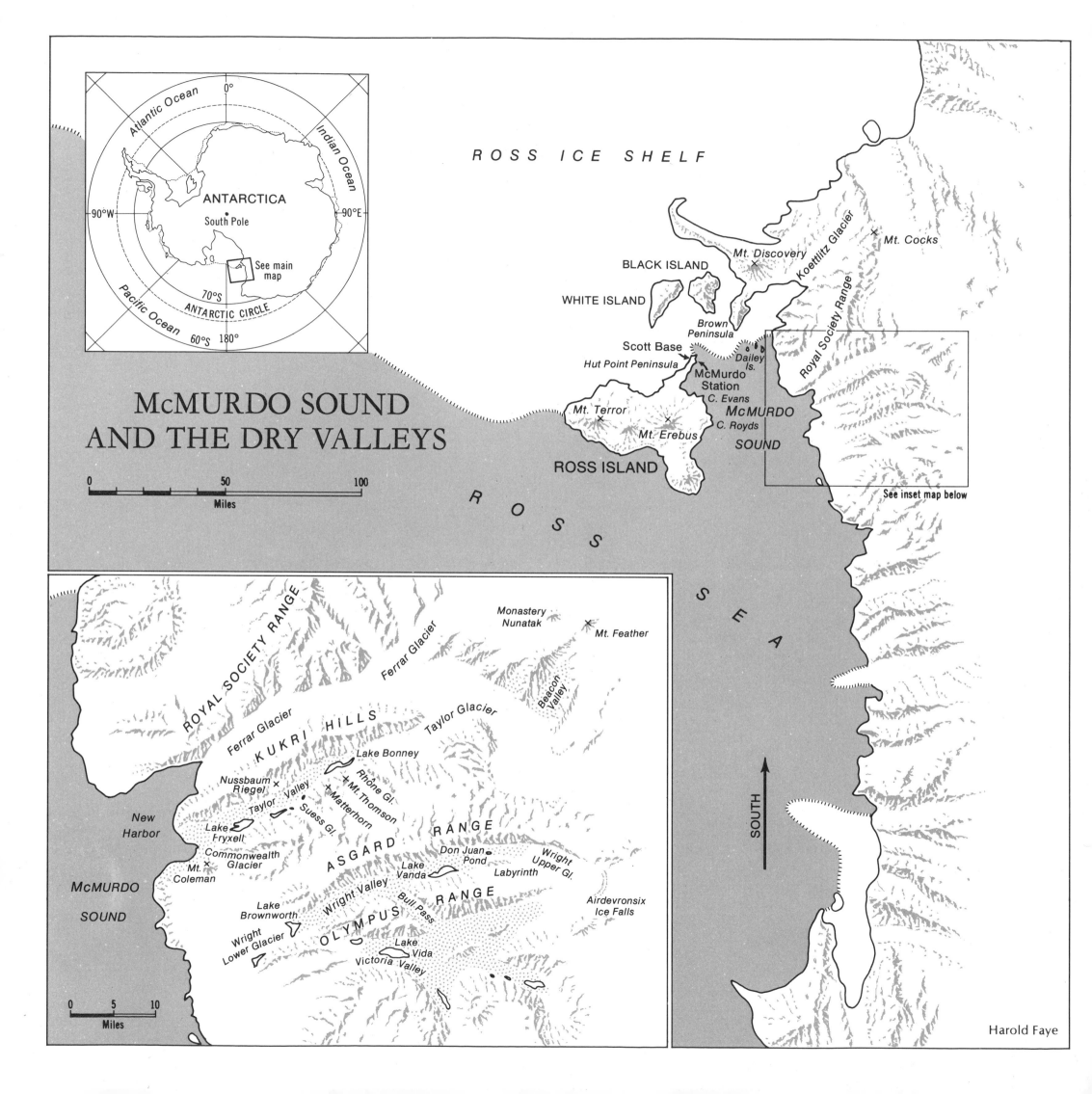

ROSS ICE SHELF

ROSS SEA

McMURDO SOUND
AND THE DRY VALLEYS

Atlantic Ocean
Indian Ocean
ANTARCTICA
South Pole
0°
90°W
90°E
70°S
ANTARCTIC CIRCLE
60°S
180°
Pacific Ocean
See main map

0   50   100
Miles

BLACK ISLAND
WHITE ISLAND
Mt. Discovery
Koettlitz Glacier
Mt. Cocks
Royal Society Range
Brown Peninsula
Scott Base
Hut Point Peninsula
Dailey Is.
McMurdo Station
C. Evans
McMURDO
C. Royds
SOUND
Mt. Terror
Mt. Erebus
ROSS ISLAND
See inset map below

ROYAL SOCIETY RANGE
Monastery Nunatak
Mt. Feather
Ferrar Glacier
Ferrar Glacier
Taylor Glacier
Beacon Valley
KUKRI HILLS
Lake Bonney
Nussbaum Riegel
Rhône Gl.
Mt. Thomson
Taylor Valley
Suess Gl.
Matterhorn
New Harbor
Lake Fryxell
RANGE
Commonwealth Glacier
Don Juan Pond
Wright Upper Gl.
Mt. Coleman
ASGARD
Lake Vanda
Labyrinth
McMURDO SOUND
Wright Valley
RANGE
Airdevronsix Ice Falls
Lake Brownworth
Bull Pass
OLYMPUS
Wright Lower Glacier
Lake Vida
Victoria Valley

SOUTH

0   5   10
Miles

Harold Faye

IV. McMURDO SOUND

My shoulder healed satisfactorily and by spring I had recovered nearly the full use of my arm. When the National Science Foundation offered to send me to the American base at McMurdo Sound on Ross Island during the next austral summer, I accepted eagerly. The N.S.F. also made arrangements for me to sail in January on the *Glacier* from McMurdo to Palmer Station, a 2,400-mile voyage circling the Antarctic Continent. At Palmer Station I was to join the *Hero* for her last few polar cruises of the summer. Having arranged to spend a few weeks in New Zealand on my way to Antarctica, on November 12 I boarded a Military Air Command C141 cargo plane at Point Mugu Air Force Base in California, to begin a sixteen-hour flight to Christchurch, New Zealand, with stops in Honolulu and Pago Pago, American Samoa. We lost a day in crossing the International Dateline and landed at 10:30 A.M. on November 14 at the Christchurch International Airport, twenty-one hours after taking off from Point Mugu.

From Christchurch the flight to McMurdo was set for the early morning of December 5. At six A.M. on that day I took a taxi to the airport, where I waited for the warehouse to open so that I could re-sort my baggage and put on my Antarctic weather clothes. At a quarter to nine, the C 130, a New Zealand Air Force cargo plane, took off for McMurdo. Flying time was expected to be seven or eight hours. The C 130 is the work horse of the Air Force. When seen squatting on the runway, this great, bulky four-motor propeller plane appears quite unflyable. The view inside is, if anything, less reassuring. Nevertheless, C 130s do in fact carry very large amounts of cargo for long distances. Passengers sit facing inward on web seats attached to the side of the fuselage in a continuous band. The space between the web seats and the entire rear three-quarters of the plane, as in the C 141, is filled with a huge stack of freight chained to the deck. Most of the space between the web seats, however, was reserved for personal baggage, which included all my photographic gear and whatever of the other passengers' carry-on scientific equipment could not be entrusted to the routine rough handling of the loading crews. Three small portholes on either side allowed views of the outside world—obstructed, however, by life vests and the webbing of the seat backs. There were only five civilian passengers; all the others on board were military personnel or members of the crew.

After flying three hours above unbroken overcast, we left the clouds behind and could look down on a sea covered with pack ice. The plane was now south of the Antarctic Convergence, where the cold north-moving water sinks below the warmer water of the South Pacific. The ocean was covered with pans and irregular floes of ice separated by narrow channels of blue water. From the air, the packed cakes of ice looked like a floor paved with angular blocks of white marble, reflecting the bright sun with such intensity that after a short time, turning back to the interior of the plane was like entering a dark closet.

After a while, land appeared below. The plane had crossed the Antarctic coast west of Cape Adare and was flying above a landscape where range after range of triangular black peaks projected out of a vast white plain of glacial ice, on which the low-lying sun cast deep shadows. As we flew on and on, the Ross Sea eventually appeared far away to the left, its open water much less tightly packed with sea ice than that of the north.

As we came close to McMurdo Sound, I began seeing valleys between mountain ranges that were free of snow except for hanging glaciers on the highest slopes—the dry valleys of which I had heard and which I hoped to visit. Then the plane passed over a white surface threaded with dark lines—cracks in the ice covering McMurdo Sound—and interspersed here and there by a grayish band of glacial till where the Koettlitz Glacier had spilled onto the Ross Ice Shelf. We now seemed to be descending rapidly, and before long with a slight bump we touched down and came to a stop. We had landed on the ice runway on McMurdo Sound, used by wheeled planes from September to December.

A Holmes and Narver representative, who met me in a red Ford pickup fitted with enormous tires, showed me to my quarters in the ''Hotel,'' the dormitory where most of the scientists were staying. My roommate was Tom Kellogg, a University of Maine geologist. He was an associate of George Denton, a professor of glacial geology at the same university, whom I met the next day and with whom I shared a love of the coast of Maine. Denton knew my book *Summer Island*. During the next few weeks I was to see a great deal of George Denton and his party.

McMurdo Station is an untidy complex made up of a hundred or so buildings surrounded by storage yards, power lines, and military and civilian vehicles of all kinds—including trucks, bulldozers and Nodwells, fire engines, and motorized fork lifts, most of them with no place to go beyond the few acres of the station. The largest community on the continent, McMurdo has a summer population of about 800, counting administration, transportation, maintenance, and communication personnel along with the scientists whose work they support. With its muddy streets, its trash and garbage dumps, and the heaps of smashed machines and disabled vehicles that are inevitable where salvage is impossible, the station suggests a military depot in wartime. It is located just north of Cape Armitage, the southernmost extremity of Ross Island. A little more than a mile away, on the eastern side of the same peninsula, is Scott Base, the New Zealand station. At the base of Cape Armitage, a steep pyramid of rock called Observation Hill rises between the two stations to a narrow summit several hundred feet high. Here the New Zealanders have erected a tall cross in memory of Scott and his companions who perished on their return from the Pole. Twenty-four miles north by east from the McMurdo base, the gleaming white mass of Mt. Erebus towers to a scarcely believable height of over 12,000 feet. Erebus, an active volcano, was in eruption at the time of its discovery by Ross and again during Scott's visit; a white plume of vapor and smoke perennially floats in the pale blue sky above its unseen crater. Mountaineers who have ascended to the summit, and pilots who have flown directly over it, have reported a glowing body of molten rock within its volcano's recesses. A party of French volcanists who attempted to descend into the crater were driven out by a sudden ejection of sulphurous fumes.

On the day after my arrival I went to see Chris Shepherd, the chief administrator for the National Science Foundation, at his office in a building, known as the Chalet because of its architectural style, which serves as the scientific center for the base. Shepherd asked me to list all the places I wished to see and everything I wanted to photograph, and I proceeded to do so, in consultation with scientists who were familiar with Antarctica.

On the next day—a Sunday, and thus a holiday for military personnel and helicopter pilots—I made arrangements to visit Scott's first hut, less than a mile from McMurdo, which the New Zealanders maintain as a historic monument. Inside the low, rectangular, hip-roofed building, everything remains just as it was in 1902—the cooking area with its iron stove and raised platform for eating above the cold floor; the storage area containing some of the original tins of Huntley and Palmer biscuits, a rusting candle lantern, and—a macabre detail suggesting hasty departure—an opened tin of time-blackened sardines.

When Ernest Shackleton, who had been evacuated from Scott's first Antarctic expedition after he came down with scurvy, returned with an expedition of his own in 1907, he had originally planned to occupy the camp on Hut Point; but after Scott announced his intention to use the hut himself, Shackleton established a camp at Cape Royds, twenty-five miles farther north on Ross Island. When Scott returned in 1910, he set up a camp at Cape Evans. Like Scott's own first base, these two huts are now maintained as monuments to the two leaders. Later on during my stay, I made arrangements for a visit to both huts with Chris Shepherd. We stopped first at Cape Evans. Outside the weathered wooden building, bales of hay for Scott's ponies remained stacked, still intact, and pony harnesses still hung in the open stalls adjoining the hut. Piled against the wall were crates of tinned food, which were beginning to come apart, spilling their contents of rusting cans. Near an empty kennel lay the mummified remains of a dog, a heavy leather collar with a rusted chain still fastened around its shriveled neck. The skin on the dog's head had shrunk away, exposing the skull and the white teeth in a snarling grimace. Another kennel contained dog bones and a bleached skull. Whatever flesh still adhered to the bones of these pitifully emaciated creatures at the time of their death had long ago been torn off by the skuas. Were these huskies, left behind in the confusion of departure when the rescue party arrived, to die a lingering death of starvation, or had they been mercifully killed? The record is not clear.

In the dark interior of the hut, the two-tier bunks still held stiff, unwieldy sealskin sleeping bags—with the fur inside—in crumpled disarray. At one end of the large room, the cast-iron stove that served for heating and cooking looked so new and functional that it might just have been installed. On the cupboard shelves were dishes, preserved foods, and spices of all kinds, their labels still bright and readable after sixty years. A table in front of one window held an assortment of chemical equipment—test tubes, stands, alcohol burners, and glass-stoppered reagent bottles. On another table were the corroding components of a primitive wireless set. A photographic darkroom occupied the far end of the hut opposite the door. Fur-lined boots and shoes stood in neat pairs where their owners had last removed them. A framed photograph of King George V and Queen Mary, hung against a well-lighted partition near the center of the room, had begun to fade. The lingering aura of that departed company, of men who had perished and of those survivors who had waited, virtual prisoners within these walls through the long winter months, still haunted the place.

Shackleton's hut on Cape Royds had much the same air of hurried abandonment, of eagerness to leave behind every reminder of the months endured there. From this spot, his headquarters when he tried for the Pole in 1907–9, he had arrived within eighty miles of his goal—only to turn back because his rations were on the point of giving out, and barely surviving even so.

Near Shackleton's hut is a rookery of Adélie penguins, the southernmost of all bird nesting grounds. It is off limits to visitors except those with a compelling reason for visiting it, since in recent years the population has declined as a result of predation by skuas, aggravated by human disturbance which frightens the adults from their eggs and young and exposes them to attack.

On the afternoon of my visit to Scott's first hut, with three staff members I drove in a wide-tired pickup truck along the eastern edge of the Ross Ice Shelf to a point where crevasses in a glacier had roofed over to form ice caves. Our guide through the caves was a "Kiwi" (the standard nickname for a New Zealander) who served as an instructor at a survival school on the shelf below the glacier. The caves where the sun struck them were curtained with dripping icicles, and deep in the blue interior ice stalactites hung from the roof, furry with hoarfrost and rosetted with fragile plates and needlelike formations, all crystallized from the super-saturated air.

My first helicopter ride across McMurdo Sound was to South Stream on the shore of Bernacchi Bay, as a guest of the Denton party. South Stream during the warmest months is a small trickle from the Wilson Piedmont Glacier. While Denton and his students went off to make surveys of ancient stream deltas formed when the Ross Ice Shelf extended into the dry valleys, I took photographs along the shore, where the ice of the Sound comes into contact with the land and is crumpled by the pressure of wind and tide.

The sea ice that covers McMurdo Sound for some twenty or thirty miles north of Ross Island was beginning to thin and break up, and I was told that open water was much closer than it had been on this date for several years. The cracks that were opening up allowed penguins to advance south, and with them came the Weddell seals and killer whales. From the air on the return trip from South Stream I could see the dark, elliptical bodies of seals lying along the wider breaks. In places where a rift had refrozen, the seals kept round holes open, from which their tracks radiated like the spokes of a wheel, each track a wide continuous ribbon with flipper imprints on either side. Scattered about the entire area, the bodies of basking seals looked like dark slugs. Penguin tracks were also visible, as parallel dotted lines spreading away from the holes in all directions, to form a black, weblike pattern. As the helicopter descended following a brief landing on Marble Point, we could see the trails of separate three-toed, backward-pointing prints left by individual penguins.

The noise of the machine caused panic among the birds, who scurried away from under us to all sides, some towards the open water and others away from it. They ran with flippers extended like wings, which indeed they are in a sense, and when they stumbled and fell on their faces they continued to toboggan along on their bellies. One group of Adélies plunged all at once into an open waterhole. There were also emperor penguins—unmistakable, even at a considerable distance, because of their long necks and bills and their swaying gait. They did not appear to panic as the Adélies had done, but perhaps that was only because they are larger birds and unable to move so fast. Some groups I saw were hurrying along, all swaying in unison from side to side as though in a comic ballet. A few of the seals were also alarmed by the noise and caterpillared towards open water with surprising speed.

A behavior study of Weddell seals was being conducted at Hutton Cliffs, ten miles north of the station, where a permanent rift in the sea ice parallel to the cliffs allowed the seals to maintain breathing holes through which they could enter the sea to feed. Since the female seals were beginning to wean their pups and disperse, the project would soon end for the season. But there was still time for me to photograph the seals, and I was flown there early in the morning. Two members of the team showed me around. Their equipment included sound-recording devices and an underwater cable television camera for observing the seals under the ice. The bull seals guarded their harems and defended their territories, fighting off all male intruders from under the rift in the ice—an activity that kept them in the water most of the time. The females lay on the ice for long periods, returning to the water only to feed. Many of the mother seals looked emaciated. A few of the younger pups that were still nursing wore the black lanugo fur coats with which they were born, but which would be replaced by the mottled coarser adult hair as they matured. Young seals grow fat on the rich milk of their mothers, adding weight at the rate of five pounds a day from a birth weight of sixty. They are taught how to swim and how to come to the surface to breathe.

Seals on the ice, especially the young, keep up an incessant, sheeplike bleating and baaing. These sounds, however, are only a small part of their vocal repertory. As I stood beside a somnolent mother Weddell whose pup had just left her to slide head first down a black hole in the ice, and puzzled over her extreme lethargy and indifference to my intrusion—so unlike the behavior of the seals I had encountered in the Antarctic the year before—I became conscious of a musical trill that seemed to have no one point of origin but rather in some mysterious way to pervade the surroundings. Then the sounds changed to a series of muffled peeps and chirps and became focussed, unbelievably, underneath the ice in front of me. While I asked myself whether there could be some strange Antarctic fish capable of vocalizing as certain tropical species do, I became aware that the sounds were being answered from closer at hand. The female Weddell beside me was uttering soft trills and gurgles, which soon gave way in quality to harsher, more strident notes, rising into a shrill whistle and then ending, most incongruously, with a belch. These sounds by their variety seemed to have no significance as specific communication, but rather to constitute a general announcement of being there and feeling good—the same function, in short, as the joyous singing they so much resembled.

Most of the pups were playing together in and out of the water, more in it than otherwise. While one pup lay on the ice with its head hanging over the edge of a breathing hole, another would surface in the black water, its wet fur sleek and dark, the outline of a round head and blunt, whiskered muzzle made visible by shiny highlights as the two animals sniffed and nuzzled each other. The seal on the ice would then slip into the water and both would vanish beneath the dark surface. One or two heads might reappear minutes later, but could easily escape notice if you were not watching closely. The first sign that a seal was returning to the surface was the sound of its breathing; then, at a far corner in the rift first a circle of ripples and then a pair of large, limpid eyes would appear. Because several pups shared the same breathing holes, identification could be made only when one pup crawled out and approached its mother. A few pups were accepted by their mothers and allowed to suckle. Most were being weaned and would be rebuffed with a snarl.

In the afternoon I accompanied the research team on an excursion a mile out on the ice, where a group of unmated female Weddells were distributed along a narrow rift; here they maintained holes that gave them access to the sea. Although they seemed undisturbed by either our presence or the noise of the vehicle that brought us, their equanimity was soon to be shattered. The purpose of the visit was to learn the current stage of the estrous cycle in a sampling of these females. Their capture, using ropes to draw a heavy canvas hood over the head of the animal, was easier when carried out by surprise. If a first attempt failed, the operation became a lively gymnastic confrontation between the leaping manipulators of the hood and a frantically twisting half-ton seal. With the hood finally in place the animal became strangely quiet, either lulled or frightened by her suddenly claustral state. Once a vaginal smear had been deftly taken and the hood removed, the indignant creature would make for the security of her adopted medium, plunging into the nearest breathing hole.

After the breeding season ends in December, as the increasing warmth of the austral summer sun softens and melts the sea ice in McMurdo Sound, cracks develop and widen to produce long rifts of open water. These open rifts occur up to the very edge of the McMurdo Ice Shelf, around the circumference of Hut Point Peninsula, and westward to the Dailey Islands. Even before the widenings have progressed beyond narrow slots, seals and penguins discover and use them for ready access to the water of the sound. When the rifts become wider, families of killer whales move in. They cruise back and forth, from time to time rising perpendicularly out of the water to a height of from six to eight feet, surveying the surface of the ice for the seals and penguins that are their prey. (They feed as well on the abundant bottom-dwelling fish.) From a helicopter, one can see the narrower cracks and circular breathing holes used by the seals and penguins. Those that have been in use longest have been worn almost perfectly round by the bodies sliding in and out, and by the seals' habit of biting off the ice edge to keep it from freezing over.

When killer whales appear in the leads, penguins stay on the surface, clustered on the edge of the ice as they wait for the whales to pass. They seem to know when it is safe to enter the water and then plunge in all together, splashing about like boys in a swimming hole—only to shoot out again at the first indication of danger, which they are able to detect before it is evident to a person standing nearby.

Aside from leopard seals—which, however, do not penetrate into McMurdo Sound, but which elsewhere are by far the most serious menace faced by Antarctic penguins—the less abundant killer whales are the only mammalian predators of the Antarctic seas. Largest of the genus *Phocaena*, which includes the porpoises, the killer whale or orca is a kind of superpredator that goes, often in packs, after whatever swims—including other whales and all the Antarctic pinnipedians, with the possible exception of mature elephant seals. Killer whales' stomachs have been found to contain a dozen whole seals at once. With the breakup of the sea ice in summer they move into McMurdo Sound to feed on the rich marine life of the continental shelf, including both seals and penguins. But nowhere on the vast Antarctic Continent has any land mammal ever evolved or become established.

V. THE DRY VALLEYS

Before leaving for Antarctica I had been told that the ice-free valleys of the Transantarctic Mountains would be a rich source of photographic subjects. This range extends along the western shore of the Ross Sea, all the way from Cape Adare to the Ross Ice Shelf. The so-called dry valleys that transect it are mainly concentrated at the end facing Ross Island. Most of them are blocked at either end by a massive glacier, and smaller glaciers descend into them partway from either side. When they became ice-free, and why they remain so, have been subjects of absorbing concern to geologists and glaciologists ever since Scott's first expedition discovered and explored Taylor Valley in 1902–4. I was fortunate in that Dr. George Denton invited me to accompany his team of geologists on several occasions. An authority on glacial geology, Dr. Denton had been coming to Antarctica for seventeen years. He was able to suggest a large number of places that I found well worth visiting.

Besides the wildlife of the continent, I had hoped to photograph ice and snow formations wherever accessible, as well as the geological phenomena of the dry valleys. After I had given my list to Chris Shepherd, he worked out a schedule for me. Except for short distances overland or on fixed sea ice, where motorized vehicles or sledges are used, transportation in the Antarctic is almost entirely by helicopter. I had ten hours of helicopter flying time allotted to me—a total that counted only the time actually spent in the air, and which could be augmented by invitations to go along with another group when space was available.

My first visit to the dry valleys was on December 10, 1975, when I accompanied the Denton party to the foot of Taylor Valley. The helicopter dropped us on the lower slopes of Mt. Coleman not far from the frozen surface of New Harbor, a wide embayment in the coast. My goal was to walk three miles inland to Commonwealth Glacier. At first George Denton didn't want me to go alone because of my inexperience, but he finally relented, providing me with an elephant's foot (a half-length sleeping·bag lined with down, for keeping the legs and lower body warm) to be used in the event of an incapacitating injury, and a smoke bomb for attracting a search helicopter. Except for short periods and in circumsribed areas, going anywhere alone in the Antarctic is strictly against regulations.

As I set off across a series of boulder-strewn morainic ridges, the glacier was not visible; and from the crest of each rocky moraine, another and higher moraine came into view, still blocking the sight I hoped for. As the shore retreated behind me, the desolation seemed to multiply with the distance. This was the loneliest, most silent place I had ever entered; the only sounds were the wind blowing against my parka and the tripod I carried, and the faint buzz of my own circulation, like the hum of distant insects. My heavy camera, which I carried in a backpack, made the ascent of the moraines, where with each step forward I slid half a step back, especially tiring.

When at last I saw the glacier, it seemed a long way off, separated from me as it was by a wide stretch of lower moraines. As I plodded on, with my nose dripping and my vision obscured by the fur edge of my parka hood, which I had pulled down so low over my head, to shut out a strong cross wind, that I could see only a few feet, I thought about the warnings I had received against overconfidence and against underestimating the dangers of Antarctic travel. Finally, however, I came to the last moraine. Between it and the ice cliff lay a trough, a sort of catch basin for chunks of ice and snow that from time to time broke away from the ice wall.

In places the bottom of the trough was covered with a sheet of green discolored ice. Rising almost directly out of this frozen pond, the perpendicular face of the glacier towered upward for a hundred feet, festooned with icicles but otherwise as smooth in texture as though a gigantic blowtorch had been swept quickly across it and then withdrawn.

The moraine on which I now stood appeared not to have been produced by this glacier but rather by an ancient, much larger one that filled Taylor Valley. The lobe of Commonwealth Glacier, the largest of the valley's lateral glaciers, is five miles in circumference from where it squeezes between Mt. Coleman and Mt. Falconer to reach the bottom of the valley.

The walk back seemed less long and was less exhausting than the one out, partly because I took a higher route and thereby avoided the steepest ridges. The entire distance was scarcely more than seven miles, and I was back at the rendezvous point before the Denton party arrived.

This first day was no more than an introduction to the stupendous geological processes that are revealed in the exposed rocks of the mountain ranges. I was eager to see more and to visit the far reaches of these valleys, so important for an understanding of Antarctic geology. Within the area that contains them, covering roughly fifty square miles, are subsidiary ranges, oriented approximately at right angles to the Trans-Antarctic Mountains and dividing it into this series of troughs that are partially ice-free. The mountains that make up these ranges are heavily glaciated around their peaks, which rise to heights of 2000 meters and from which ice tongues descend towards the valley floor. Their names were given by the first explorers: the Kukri Hills, the Asgard Range, the Olympus Range, and the St. Johns Range. South of the Kukri Hills, and separated from them by the Ferrar Glacier, is the Royal Society Range (with peaks over 3,000 meters).

Taylor, the first dry valley to be discovered, lies between the Kukri Hills and the Asgard Range. It is the only dry valley that is ice-free at its lower end, where it borders on McMurdo Sound.

In lower Taylor Valley is a frozen lake, which has been named Mummy Pond because of the large number of mummified seals that have been found along its shore. These brown, desiccated remains are to be found elsewhere in the dry valleys, mainly close to the sea ice but miles from it as well. Lying exposed on the gravel floors of the valleys where the living creature had succumbed to starvation and exposure, the carcasses are usually intact, indicating that scavengers did not discover them—not even the ubiquitous skuas associated with penguin rookeries and human garbage dumps. Many of the seals appear to have been young animals, leading some scientists to argue that they had become separated from the colony, lost their way, and wandered inland until failing strength ended the struggle. Others maintain that they must have belonged to a population that inhabited the western shore of McMurdo Sound at a time when the climate was warmer and when the sea, then at a higher level, extended far into the dry valleys. Carbon-14 dating, which has established the age of some but not all of the carcasses at several thousand years, gives support to the second theory.

Among the most spectacular features of the dry valleys are the glacier tongues that descend from both sides. Many of these reach nearly to the valley floor, and three of them extend across it. What makes these glaciers unique to the Antarctic—with the possible exception of a few in northern Greenland and one high in the Bolivian Andes—is a perpendicular ice front that may be anywhere from fifty to a hundred feet high. Such sharply defined walls of ice are a feature of advancing glaciers. In Antarctica, however, that advance is extremely slow because the glaciers are frozen to the bedrock on which they rest. What little creeping that occurs is compensated by the melting and sublimation, in the dry air of the Antarctic summer, of the fragments that fall from the vertical ice fronts so that they do not accumulate.

LABYRINTH, WRIGHT VALLEY

CINDER CONE, TAYLOR VALLEY

Scientists have prospected for minerals in the "dry valleys" since the time of Scott and Shackleton.

WRIGHT VALLEY

This dry valley was discovered in the summer of 1904 by members of the Scott expedition as they were returning from a trip up Ferrar Glacier and onto the polar ice sheet.

CAVERNOUS EROSION, BULL PASS, OLYMPUS RANGE

DON JUAN POND, WRIGHT VALLEY

The name was probably a whim of a geologist.

REMNANTS OF WRIGHT LOWER GLACIER

VENTIFACTS, STONES WORN AND POLISHED BY
WINDBLOWN SAND, WRIGHT VALLEY

MUMMIFIED SEAL WITH SKIN PARTIALLY INTACT

The first expedition to discover mummified seals in the Antarctic was led by H. J. Bull, who reasoned that the polar climate could not support land mammals, or the dead seals would have been eaten.

SHACKLETON'S WIRELESS

SHACKLETON'S STOVE, CAPE ROYDS, ROSS ISLAND

ONE OF SCOTT'S DOGS, CAPE EVANS, ROSS ISLAND

Scott's attitude towards dogs, which contributed to the tragic outcome of his polar expedition, is evident from his journal. "Bit by bit," he wrote, "I am losing all faith in them. I am afraid they will never go the pace we look for." It was from a hut at Cape Evans that Scott and his party set out on their tragic expedition to the South Pole in the winter of 1911–12.

SHACKLETON'S SUPPLIES, 1907–9

Shackleton's list of supplies "for the Shore Party for two years," 1907–9, included "6720 lb Colman's wheaten flour, 6000 lb Various tinned meat, 1000 lb York hams, 1400 lb Wiltshire bacon, etc."

KING EDWARD VII AND QUEEN ALEXANDRA, SHACKLETON'S HUT

The differing styles of expedition commanders was noted by Sir Edmund Hillary, who accompanied Sir Vivian Fuchs on his first crossing of the Antarctic continent, in 1955–58: "For scientific discovery, give me Scott; for speed and efficiency of travel give me Amundsen; but when disaster strikes and all hope is gone, get down on your knees and pray for Shackleton."

Where these glaciers spill over a steep ridge of rock high on a mountainside, the ice breaks into fragments that fall clear of the outcrop, accumulating in such quantity that they coalesce at its base. The solid mass thus formed then begins to flow like the parent glacier; known as a reconstructed glacier, it is readily identified by the precipice of exposed rock that divides it from its source above. Another curious glacial phenomenon is the rock glacier, found only in the colder parts of the world. It is composed of ice and of the rock fragments that accumulate in terminal moraines or as talus below steep mountain slopes. As these become cemented together by compaction with snow and freezing water, they move in the same way as a glacier. The moisture contained in the upper layers of gravel deposits—old moraines and deltas—becomes a permafrost which, under the influence of moderate temperature changes brought about by the summer sun, becomes marked by a network of grooves, most clearly visible from the air, and known to geologists as nonsorted or sand-wedge polygons. Caused by freezing and contraction, these polygons vary in size from a few feet to as much as twelve yards across.

During the warmest months, when on windless sunny days the temperature rises above freezing, a certain amount of melting takes place. Moats develop around frozen lakes where the ice makes contact with the heat-absorbing shore; water flows off north-facing glacial fronts and forms icicles; and rivulets are produced wherever sun-warmed sand and gravel touch the ice. Wright Lower Glacier, an offshoot of the massive Wilson Piedmont Glacier, which occupies the edge of the continent for a stretch of more than thirty miles, and fills the lower end of Wright Valley, is the only retreating glacier in the dry valleys. Remnants of this glacier, sculptured by melting into glistening translucent peaks, spires, and bizarre shapes suggesting those of animals, stand like grounded icebergs in a sea of yellow sand. Meltwater flows in braided streams down shallow gullies from the terraced wall of ice towards a frozen lake that wraps around the glaciers' front edge. At its northern end this is not a continuous single body of water, but is broken up by a jumble of sand-covered ice mounds, ridges, and glacial fragments into a series of narrow parallel ponds. The area occupied by these ponds, known collectively as Lake Brownworth, was at one time covered by Wright Lower Glacier; now the ice has melted back more than a mile. Unlike most of the other dry-valley glaciers, the front of Wright Glacier is not abruptly perpendicular but slopes back in a sequence of terraced steps that are deeply gullied and eroded. The great quantities of sand that overlie older glacial till is another indication of retreat. Wherever the sand was probed by ice ax, ice was found underneath. Sand washed down from higher levels fills pockets and depressions, to protect the underlying ice from melting. The exposed blocks and pinnacles of ice melt faster, eventually becoming new pockets which then fill with sand from the formerly depressed areas. Thus a constant alternation between sand-covered and sand-free ice takes place as melting progresses.

Along the western border of Lake Brownworth, where the helicopter set us down, an old moraine slopes upward out of the valley. It is covered with wind-shaped and wind-polished stones—known as ventifacts—of all sizes. Below the slope, where a flat stretch beside the lake has accumulated a desert pavement of pebbles, a few large stones lie scattered, similarly polished by the wind and sand of hundreds, perhaps even thousands of years.

The Olympus Range, a narrow ridge of peaks bearing names from Greek mythology, lies parallel to the Asgard mountains and forms the northern boundary of Wright Valley. Unlike the Asgards, which are more than ten miles wide and contain icefields from which glacial tongues extend north and south down the slopes of Wright and Taylor valleys, the Olympus Range contains few glaciers. Except for small pockets of ice and snow, they are naked masses of rock whose geological structure is revealed in the bedded strata of sandstones, doleritic intrusions, and dyking. Next to the Olympus Range is a roughly triangular desert basin, known as Victoria Valley, which extends north for fifteen miles and encompasses a group of short ravines that fan out from the perpetually frozen face of Lake Vida. This gleaming white ellipse is set off by dark moraine gravels and stream deposits, which cover much of the valley floor and rise in rolling slopes from all sides of the lake shore—a much eroded and weathered record left behind by the ice sheet that occupied the valley long ago. Over thousands of years, wind and frost have worn down these old deposits into a closely packed pavement of basaltic stones. Fierce buffeting winds, carrying blast after blast of fine abrasive sand, have fluted and polished the black oxidized basalt until its multiform facets glitter like mirrors in the sun. These ventifacts have been smoothed equally on all sides; many of the smaller ones are shaped into little pyramids.

Bull Pass, a broad sloping plain named for an early explorer, reaches up onto the Olympus Range from Mckelvey Valley, one of the depressions that feed into Lake Vida. Narrowing as it ascends to a summit under the western side of Mt. Orestes, the pass ends with a precipitous dropoff into the watercourse of Onyx River, flowing through Wright Valley. Littering the pass are granite boulders, some weighing thousands of tons. Although the question of whether they are glacial erratics or have some other origin is in dispute, they are interesting for other reasons. Since they came to rest, a very long time ago, they have been subject to erosive forces that have carved them into fantastic shapes by what geologists call the tafoni process—a cavernous weathering caused by the action of salts. Granite, a metamorphic rock composed of discrete crystals of various minerals, is especially subject to this kind of disintegration. Minute amounts of dehydrated salts lodge in the interstices between crystals; then with a change in atmospheric humidity they take up water, expand, and pop off crystal grains from the rock. In this way, a granite boulder exposed to the weather is ultimately reduced to a heap of coarse sand. Cavernous weathering seems to progress more rapidly on protected surfaces. As decomposition proceeds, these surfaces become concave and thus still more protected, so that the tafoni process is favored still more. The results are dramatically evident on Bull Pass. Medium-sized boulders have been hollowed out to resemble giant clamshells or a monster's gaping mouth. Others have become so thinned by interior sculpting that holes work through to the opposite side. A boulder that appears fairly substantial may turn out to be only a thin shell of rock concealing a hollow interior. Sharp spines and flat planes of stone, with all manner of delicate tracery, are everywhere in this amazing sculpture garden, where there are many pieces reminiscent of the works of Henry Moore. One mass of granite suggested a huge blob of melting wax, and another an enormous winged creature about to take flight. Surrounding all these vast monoliths are drifts of coarse yellow sand, the indestructible product of their decay and the raw material of future strata.

Where Bull Pass turns down towards Wright Valley and immediately above the steep dropoff to the Onyx River, the granite bedrock has been eroded into pyramidal towers so closely and regularly spaced that they still touch at the base. From fifteen to twenty feet high, these towers are composed of randomly stepped horizontal slabs piled into a diminishing, cairnlike structure crowned by a single cap rock, and suggesting a stratification disrupted by vertical fracturing and water erosion.

From Bull Pass we flew first to the New Zealand weather station on Lake Vanda in Wright Valley, and from there to Don Juan Pond, twelve miles up the valley's south fork. The pond fills a pocket in the valley floor, which is closed at the upper end by a brooding rock glacier, and confined narrowly on both sides by walls of gray scree—a scene of gloom and foreboding, lifeless as the moon itself. Half the area is a mud flat covered with salt, which gives its surface a dusted look ,and it was here that our helicopter landed. The pond's shallow waters, which merge gradually into this mixture of dried salt and mud, are a saturated solution of calcium chloride. Scattered erratically over the entire area are large and small granite boulders, the larger of which have been sculptured by the tafoni process. Around each rock is a moist slight depression, filled with crystals of the hexahydrate of calcium chloride, an exceedingly hygroscopic mineral to which a Japanese mineralogist has given the name *antarcticite*. At higher temperatures the crystals go quickly into solution and therefore must be refrigerated for preservation. Death Valley, California, is the only other place in the world where a comparable situation is found.

VI. EXPLORING THE ICE

In the high Antarctic latitudes of McMurdo Sound and Ross Island, where life is minimal, the scenery consists entirely of land forms that reveal the sequence of primordial geological events. To a trained eye the tectonic forces that have shaped the continents are manifest in the dykes and faults and folded strata exposed on bare ridges and escarpments, in ash and cinder cones, and in the flows of lava from long extinct volcanoes; and the working of the still active forces is clear in the heaped glacial moraines, sandy deltas, boulder-strewn talus, and eroded ocean cliffs.

Between land and frozen sea is a region of instability and confusion where the tides and freezing cold are in competition. Here uplifting and subsidence, contraction and expansion produce a chaotic jumble of both elements. Blocks of ice, white with bubbles of captured air, are squeezed up through deposits of muddy sand tinted olive green by algae. Interspersed among them are ponds of pure translucent blue ice, the frozen inroads of the sea. As one walks away from shore through this chaos the scene gradually changes. The farther out from land that the sand has been carried, the more it shows the overlayering of ice by an intermittent process: heated by the sun, the sand slowly melts its way down and settles into pockets that unite beneath the surface, leaving above a reticulated lacy roof of ice supported by many small pillars. Surface melting produces a fringe of icicles that hang from the edges of the reticulum. The ponds of blue sea ice become larger the farther they are from shore; but forces pressing from below mound their surfaces into thin white plates that crack apart and stand on edge. I photographed these strange phenomena of the contact between land and sea for two days—first on the shore of New Harbor and then at a marine biologists' camp, where a diving hole had been blasted a mile out on the ice.

Fresh-water ice on ponds and lakes, although quite different from seashore ice, likewise occurs in a variety of distinct forms. Most lakes are frozen to a smooth surface of transparent or semitransparent blue ice. Often bands tinted in varying shades of blue occur, marking the amount of snow incorporated in the surface—or perhaps they may be the result of temporary melting and refreezing.

Southwest of Ross Island, jutting from the continent into the Ross Ice Shelf, is a peninsula from which the naked rock cone of Mt. Discovery ascends to a height of nearly 2,700 meters. A few miles to the east of Mt. Discovery, due south of the McMurdo base, lie two volcanic islands surrounded by the Ross Ice Shelf—one snow-covered, the other bare dark rock—that have been named White Island and Black Island respectively. The Ross shelf sweeping between Mt. Discovery and Black Island to become the McMurdo Ice Shelf, picks up a great burden of morainic rubble and carries it out past the sea's edge. Here, the small cinder cones that form the Dailey Islands block its advance, so that the glacial till is dumped onto the sea ice. Because of the large amounts of morainic material set down there on top of the intermingled ice of sea and shelf, the region around the Dailey Islands is known as the dirty ice. Extending north from Mt. Discovery is a thumb-shaped headland, the Brown Peninsula. It serves to lock the Koettlitz Glacier, which originates near the southern end of the Royal Society Range, against the eastern shore of the continent. From an icefield at the foot of Mt. Cocks, this glacier is forced through a narrow pass to debouch into the western bay of McMurdo Sound, between the Dailey Islands and Brown Peninsula on the east and the mainland on the west. A branch of the Koettlitz flows into Walcott Bay, to the north of Heald Island, before dropping precipitously over a hidden barrier and re-uniting with the main glacial stream. Here, with a minimum of crevassing, ice faulting has produced a series of huge, intermeshing, icicle-hung terraces.

I had been told of a spot (off Cape Hodgson on the north side of Black Island), where in the ice ridges between the bands of glacial till, desiccated frozen sponges could be found. From the ocean bottom that had been their habitat, they had been detached by a process peculiar to polar regions: as sea water cools below the freezing point, a gradient develops, the coldest water lying on the bottom. After freezing there around any projecting objects, the ice becomes increasingly buoyant, breaking loose and floating to the surface with a cargo of objects torn from the bottom. As gradually these captured inclusions are transferred upward by a process of accretion from below and depletion at the top, they finally arrive at the surface.

When I visited Cape Hodgson along with Tom Kellogg and Sergei Barkov, a visiting Russian scientist, we found several sponges. One was frozen to the side of an ice wall from which it projected like a sconce of dry, forgotten flowers, completely freed, except at its point of attachment, from the ice by which it had once been enclosed, but still hung with dripping icicles. The remains of another large sponge lay on ice-free scree. Of the multitudinous organisms that had made up the living condominium, not a trace remained but their glassy skeletons, forming what looked like white skeins of the finest siliceous hair. All their fibrous and gelatinous constituents had long since disintegrated. I had been warned about handling these sponges; the fine spicules of silica can easily penetrate an ungloved hand.

Early in the afternoon the helicopter that had dropped us off returned and lifted us to the Koettlitz Glacier. On the way to the ice faults near Heald Island we passed over an area that presented, from a thousand feet above, a fascinating, seemingly uniform but never repetitive pattern of frozen cobalt ponds imbedded in a dimensionless network of black till and white ice. From our altitude all awareness of perspective was lost; the ridges of ice and mounds of gravel became mere lines and bands in a kaleidoscopic design.

Among the ice faults our enthusiastic and undeterred pilot found a level and relatively flat place where he was able to set the helicopter down. The surface was so slippery that a landing on a windy day would have been unwise; fortunately the air was calm. Equipped with crampons as a precaution against falling on the icy slopes, I was able to carry my heavy camera almost anywhere. In many places a thin surface sheet that crackled underfoot like breaking glass was separated by an air pocket from the hard blue ice beneath it. Perpendicular walls of ice were overhung by cornices curtained with icicles that had been fluted by melting; where they were shaded from the sun, they were thickly coated with hoarfrost. Tapering to nothing at the points of intersection with other walls they formed a system of sloping terraces that extended all the way to the ice falls in Walcott Bay.

The Dailey Islands are a place of transition from shelf ice to fast sea ice. The past eruptions of these volcanic cones have contributed material of their own to the rubble scraped by the glacier from the Antarctic Continent and swept seaward by the Ross shelf ice. As a result, horizontal seams of blue sea ice are sandwiched between layers of rock and cinders. In depressions between the gravel hills, pools of sea water flood layers of slushy green and blue ice, which in their turn cover still deeper deposits. Castellated glacial remnants surmount hills of ash and gravel, like the last defended redoubts on a field of battle. Immaculate ice pillars stand rooted in black cinders, outposts of the conflict between heat and freezing.

On the south side of Taylor Valley opposite the Suess Glacier is an area of manifest past geological activity. A location that George Denton had circled on his map of things I ought to see was Nussbaum Riegel—a dome-shaped hill of bare rock that has been smoothed by glaciation. This particular example of the formation is of special interest because its structure, consisting of a pale yellow stratified quartzite sandstone, tilted into a nearly vertical position, is transected by many dykes of black basalt running roughly parallel with the axis of the valley. The dykes, which are harder than the sandstone, make a grid of ridges a foot or two high that extend for the entire three-mile length of the dome. At its western end the basic formation changes to a granite-like gray rock broken into blocks that display scratches in a pattern known as chatter striation—a clear sign of glaciers at work, still plainly visible despite the rocks' subsequent polishing and grooving into ventifacts.

After a stop on Nussbaum Riegel we flew across the valley to Mt. Thomson, between the Matterhorn and Rhône Glaciers, and set down on a bench overlooking Lake Bonney. Strewn over the area were boulders of granite and metamorphosed quartzite sandstone, sculptured and hollowed by cavernous weathering. On the end of the bench above the Rhône Glacier was a cinder cone that had erupted at some time in the distant past, and behind the cone a talus of red and black cinder scree lay against the face of Mt. Thomson. Set against this dark background, the light-colored boulders took on a Stygian look, in sharp contrast to the blue vistas of the Antarctic.

On the way back to McMurdo from a visit to Cape Royds, we landed on the fast ice close to the south side of the Erebus Glacier Tongue, a five-mile extension into Erebus Bay of a Ross Island glacier, where our pilot had seen an ice cave he thought we might investigate. The mouth of the cave was fringed with icicles and half concealed behind a snow-covered pressure ridge. Stooping under this icy portcullis, we entered a high vaulted chamber where frosted mammillate protuberances decorated the ceiling. From this room we entered the blue, frigid core of the glacier along a crawlway that gave access to a second chamber, a crystal grotto with feathery stalactites of ice festooning a high roof so thin at its highest point that daylight was filtered in through the ice. The penumbral shade of the interior was suffused with blue, ranging from pale cerulean to the deepest indigo. The silence, isolation, and immutability of this cavern, where the process of crystallization, atom by atom, is the only change, recall forbidden sanctuaries on other continents, where mysteries of long-forgotten cults were celebrated.

For several days following this expedition, the helicopters were grounded by a whiteout. A fine snow fell intermittently, and the dim light of the sun, as it circled the horizon, was diffused through a thin high overcast. Though at evening—whose coming was signaled only by the clocks—improvement in the weather seemed imminent, for several mornings the promise was unfulfilled. On December 22, when the wind dropped and the sky became very bright, I went to bed with high hopes. On arising I was dismayed to see that the weather had reverted to white obscurity. As the morning advanced, however, the Royal Society Range began to emerge through the blanket of clouds. My flight to upper Wright Valley, originally scheduled for 9:00 A.M., finally took off at 2:00 P.M. Clouds over the Asgard and Olympus ranges looked ominous, and we landed near the New Zealand hut on Lake Brownworth after flying blind through low clouds, spiraling down through a gap that had providentially opened. Having unloaded a cargo for the New Zealand camp, we took off again into what looked like bad weather, with low clouds overhanging the valley; but then, as we approached Lake Vanda, beyond a maze of split and eroded doleritic buttes and towers known as the Labyrinth, Wright Upper Glacier shimmered into view beneath patchy clouds. A few minutes later we emerged above the Airdevronsix Icefalls into bright sunlight and cloudless skies. A recent fall of snow covered the glacier and the upper slopes of the Asgard and Olympus mountains. We circled several times in front of these rivers of crevassed and tumbling ice, which spill over the edge of the cirque that embraces the western end of Wright Upper Glacier. From above we had a view of the continental plateau, stretching endless, white, and vacant for thousands of miles. Looked at from the west, the crevasses presented an intersecting pattern of parallel rifts, their blackness all the deeper by contrast to the sheen on the snow from the westering sun.

As the helicopter alighted on the glacier in front of an ice fall, the loose new snow of the day before was swept away by the rotor's blast to uncover hard, blue, knobby ice. From close at hand the ice fall was even more awesome than from the air. Huge blue blocks were so precariously heaped one on another that they seemed ready to collapse at any moment.

The snow-laden clouds that had shrouded the Transantarctic Mountains all morning and into early afternoon had now dissipated completely; the wind dropped and temperatures rose. The good weather continued through the following day, but because it was Christmas Eve no flights were scheduled.

For a party in the lounge of the "Hotel" that evening, a live pine tree had been flown down from New Zealand and decorated with paper ornaments. The room was brightened further with tinsel rope, bells, red stockings, a paper snowman, a cardboard Santa, and a plastic poinsettia. Eggnog, hot punch, and whisky were served, accompanied by both smoked and raw Antarctic cod (*Dissosticus mawsoni*) that had been prepared by a Japanese biologist from his discarded laboratory subjects. Hamburgers were barbecued on the outside balcony, and the feast ended with a hot chocolate fondue in which fresh or frozen orange slices were to be dipped.

The surplus hamburger buns, plus some cheese, were fed to the skuas that had been attracted by the barbecue. They circled past the balcony, snatching morsels from outstretched hands (and sometimes nipping a finger), catching in midair pieces of food thrown to them, and squabbling among themselves. Temporarily satiated, they perched on the roof, peering down over the eaves like gargoyles.

Christmas Day began clear and sunny but snow fell before the day was done. Dinner in the evening was a feast, offering tenderloin steak as well as roast turkey. The snow and whiteout continued all through the next day. On December 27, when flying was resumed, I made my second trip to Bull Pass, landing in an area strewn with many large boulders. Again I was fascinated by the strangely eroded shapes, and also by the fragility of those ancient boulders, chipped away and weakened over the ages by the inexorable forces of physics and chemistry. Released grains of eroded granite lie about like chaff. Deep coves produced by these slow processes bore into the heart of the stone. No part escapes the universal leveling.

Chris Shepherd, having decided that he and other members of the N.S.F. administration would benefit by an outing, chose the afternoon of Sunday, December 28, for a six-hour close support flight to Beacon Valley and Monastery Nunatak. *Nunatak* is the Eskimo word for a mountain top surrounded by an ice sheet. Since this was a holiday for the regular helicopter crews, the commander of the VXE-6 helicopter squadron agreed to be our pilot. We stopped first near the dirty ice for a look at killer whales that we had spotted in a wide lead from overhead. We all walked over to the ice edge where the whales were spouting and swimming back and forth, and everyone took pictures. Then we flew on across the Sound and up the Ferrar Glacier to Beacon Valley.

The western wall of Beacon Valley consists of horizontal strata, yellow sandstone alternating with dark brown dolerite so as to suggest a chocolate layer cake. From the high bench where we landed after circling above the valley, we had a view to the south, where the valley divides into two box canyons. Each is a glacial cirque containing under its headwall a rock glacier, over which boulders are strewn in a series of curved, wave-like arcs for several miles down the canyon floor. The formation on which we had landed was a weakly consolidated, honey-yellow quartzite sandstone, laced with doleritic dykes—intrusive formations that are of necessity younger than the sandstone. The shelf where the helicopter stood was partly drifted over with snow. Its edge—a place to avoid—was hidden under a snow cornice of undetermined extent and thickness, which overhung a perpendicular drop of several hundred feet to the valley.

From Beacon we flew up Farnell Valley, an eastern tributary, and turned south to Monastery Nunatak. This insular mountain remnant projects above a sea of ice in the shadow of Mt. Feather on the western fringe of the Transantarctic Mountains, whose vast bulk impedes the eastward drift of the polar ice plateau. From the black basalt of the nunatak's sloping sides a fifty-foot cliff of Beacon sandstone rises sheer to a flat-topped summit, at one end of which are heaped rectangular blocks of the same stone—a formation that at first sight suggests a fortress.

Around the nunatak the ice of the polar plateau flows toward the coast, taking along a load of debris scraped from its crumbling sides, which as the two streams rejoin becomes a medial moraine. Wide where it abuts the base of the nunatak, the moraine narrows in a graceful curve out on the ice sheet, dwindling finally to a mere thread of stones and gravel.

Much to my disappointment, before we could land for a closer look Chris Shepherd received an emergency call by radio: someone at a remote station was sick, and Shepherd was needed back at McMurdo.

VII. TO THE SOUTH POLE

During the austral summer months, weather permitting, flights from McMurdo to the South Pole are made fairly often. My schedule included one planned for December 29. We left early in the morning from Williams Field, an airport on the Ross Ice Shelf five miles from McMurdo. I was invited to ride in the cockpit so that I could take photographs from the air. We had been flying over the Ross Ice Shelf for an hour and a half when the Transantarctic Mountains came into view. The first peaks were nunataks; beyond them were higher, snow-covered mountains on which many large bare slopes could be seen. The nunataks' sharply angular black peaks are interconnected by thin, curving black lines, the knifelike crests of ridges, all but buried in a coverlet of snow with the shining texture of satin. There are wrinkles in the white surface where the brittle ice that underlies it, forced up by hidden obstructions, is cracked and split. These nunataks are foothills of the range that encloses the ice cap of East Antarctica. They are loaded with glaciers that pour down from the highest elevations through valleys gouged eons ago, before Antarctica came to occupy its present position above the pole. Everywhere ice spills over and through the mountains, in small streams and in torrents dozens of miles wide and hundreds of miles long, bringing vast quantities of ice into an area of more than 100,000 square miles; half the Ross Sea is filled with it, to a depth of more than 2,000 feet.

One of these streams of ice is the Beardmore Glacier, which Scott chose as his route to the Pole. As we flew south, we crossed range after range of dark peaks deeply imbedded in white and blue ice, whose cascading ice falls passed beneath the plane for an hour—a desolate landscape, more hostile to man than any other on the planet, terrifying yet beautiful. As we neared the mountains' northern border, the peaks appeared to become smaller and more scattered (perhaps because the ice here was thicker) and the nunataks to the southwest were separated by glistening expanses of windswept, hard-packed snow. We were now passing above the featureless Antarctic ice sheet at latitude 85S—a matter of 300 miles, and an hour's flight from the South Pole. While we flew over this dreary landscape I went to sit beside the navigator at the rear of the cockpit and watch the navigation computer with its illuminated digital display of the plane's latitude and longitude. At latitude 89S I began to wonder how the machine would handle the rapid changes in longitude that would occur as the plane circled for a landing at the Pole. But I never found out; when we sighted the Pole station on the horizon, the navigator turned the computer off.

The low profile of a geodesic dome and the thin spike of a lone radio mast were all I could see on an endless plain of white. The landing field was a graded strip of snow, close enough to be within comfortable walking distance of the station even in very cold weather. Nevertheless, a Nodwell vehicle drove up to transport us up to the dome and into its dimly lighted interior. Only then did I realize how very large a building it was. Under the dome was an entire village of rectangular red structures that housed the station's various facilities—each of them an independent unit heated by water mixed with glycol from a central power plant and supplied with its water by means of a snow-melter. The interior of the dome itself was not heated and took on the ambient outdoor temperature. But it served as a shield against wind and drifting snow, which otherwise would soon have covered the smaller buildings—just as they had covered those of the old South Pole Station and thus brought about its collapse.

The station doctor and a young man named Seeley, whom I had met at the N.S.F. Asilomar conference in September, gave me a three-hour tour through the dispensary and biolab, mess hall and common room, living quarters, research laboratories for meteorology and atmospheric physics, library, and storeroom—the latter well stocked with frozen foods and bottled beverages. Extending out from the dome on opposite sides are two cylindrical quonset huts of corrugated steel—one housing the power plant, machine shop, and garage, and the other the fuel bladders, which have a capacity of 225,000 gallons of diesel oil.

My guides then suggested a visit to the old Pole station. Outside, though the sun was bright, visibility had been reduced by blowing snow in a twenty-knot wind. The official temperature that day was a relatively warm –11° Fahrenheit, but for humans there was a wind-chill factor that made it feel like 30° below zero. Because of this, we drove the few hundred yards to the old station in the Nodwell. Where it had not been graded, the surface of the plateau was covered with ridges of hard-packed snow that made the ride very bouncy. These wind-made ridges—known as snow waves or *sastrugi*, from the Russian word—can build up to several feet in height and many yards in length, and are often beautifully shaped. Any projecting object on the open plain soon develops a long sastrugos tail.

Of the old Pole station, abandoned in 1974, little was visible above the drifted snow except ventilator shafts and escape hatches. The entrance to the garage and shop, at the bottom of a twelve-foot pit, was still clear and we climbed down. Tools and equipment lay about on the floor and on benches where they had last been laid down. I was told that conditions were similar in the living quarters: dirty dishes and unemptied ash trays remained, left there by the occupants in their haste to abandon the station. In that ice-encased cold-air trap the intense cold seemed literally to suck out the warmth of my body through all its layers of arctic clothing; and eager for the tenuous warmth of the South Polar sun, I declined to explore any further. The ultimate destiny of the old Pole station, and of any subsequent establishments, is to be crushed in the polar ice cap— possibly to reappear, millennia hence, in fragments borne by calved icebergs along the coast.

On our way back to the dome we stopped briefly to look at the striped barber pole surmounted by a silvered globe and a surrounding half-circle of flags, representing each of the signatories to the Antarctic Treaty, which mark the approximate site of the geographic South Pole. In fact, since the marker was set up the drift of the ice sheet has carried it some fifty yards from the true position of the Pole—which is indicated by a bamboo stick that must be repositioned from time to time.

On the return flight, the pilot volunteered to fly at a low altitude over the Beardmore Glacier. At an altitude of 200 feet above the surface, as we skimmed along the 200-mile length of the glacier, I could see its surface structure in great detail. Vast crevassed areas stretched for miles down its length and all the way across it, from one containing mountain range to the other. Over this prodigious torrent of ice, Scott and his few men had twice dragged their sledge—for me an almost unbelievable accomplishment.

The ice shimmered in the western sun, silhouetting the mountains on our left. Snowfields here and there, at the foot of the mountains and also near their summits, shone with a specular brightness. Where the crevasses lay parallel to the course of the plane they appeared as depthless chasms, across which passage by man and sledge would be impossible. In places the crevasses were so regular and so close that they resembled the furrows in a freshly plowed field. Well down towards the foot of the glacier we passed on our right a huge snow-free gray and brown monolith that strangely resembled the Rock of Gibraltar—and indeed, the pilot told me, to flyers on the South Pole route this landmark is known as The Rock.

I had mentioned earlier during the flight that I had wanted to fly over Erebus for a view into the crater, and the pilot had offered to do so on the return to McMurdo. But as we approached Ross Island he told me we had used so much fuel in our low flight over the Beardmore that the Erebus flight would have to be canceled. Clouds were now gathering around the mountain, and I took what comfort I could in concluding that the visibility would have been poor.

The next day I was flown by helicopter to Beacon and Arena valleys and Monastery Nunatak. Tom Kellogg and several others came along for the ride. The flight started late in the morning because of unsettled weather over the Royal Society and Asgard Ranges, which worsened as the day advanced. The flight route was up the Ferrar Glacier and out over the polar plateau to Monastery Nunatak, on which I hoped we could land. But the cloud cover about the highest peaks was increasing and a strong gusty wind was blowing off the plateau. From the helicopter the top of the nunatak presented a broken, irregular surface consisting of scattered blocks of sandstone, on which any feasible landing space would be very small. Three times the crew brought the helicopter down to within a few feet of the rock, but each time the buffeting wind tossed the machine around so violently that the attempt had to be abandoned. After circling the nunatak a few times we flew off to Arena Valley, where we landed in a strong wind on a sandstone saddle that formed its southern boundary. Littering the saddle were basalt boulders, the weathered-out remnant of intrusive dykes. The wind that funneled into the valley from the south was so strong that photography with a large camera was virtually impossible. I decided not to try for any more landings here but instead to return towards McMurdo, where the weather was more clement, and to stop at the Dailey Islands before returning to base.

By the next morning the weather had improved, so that we were able to land on Monastery Nunatak despite gusty winds. The procedure for landing anywhere away from aerodromes is for the crewman to lie with his head and shoulders projecting through the open door of the helicopter so that he can see the ground below, and from there give directions to the pilot for maneuvering the ship, talking through the intercom system that connects his helmet to the pilot's. As the helicopter yawed about in the wind he talked the pilot down with simple and precise directions: "Six feet up—easy down—move two feet left—hold it—turn ten degrees right—easy down—two feet up—a little more to the right—hold it—easy down now, easy down—six inches—easy down—good on deck." But several passes and abortive attempts had to be made before the machine was safely on the rock. Later the pilot admitted that this was the hairiest landing he had ever made. When I stepped out onto the mountain top I was amazed to see how narrow the space was—scarcely large enough for the skids of the helicopter, and the only level spot. The wind was blowing a gale and very cold, but for me the view and the photographic opportunities more than justified the difficulty in landing. We did not stay long, however. During the takeoff I sat beside the open door to photograph our departure. The helicopter rose vertically for about twenty-five feet and then slowly moved forward over the sheer side of the nunatak. The sensation had a dreamlike unreality, as though the plane had been suddenly suspended over a void into which it must inevitably fall.

From Monastery Nunatak we flew north to the upper Beacon Valley, where we settled down on a rock glacier that streamed from a narrow source near the top of the headwall, sweeping down the end of the valley in a long curve that widened to a flat talus on the valley floor. The surface was completely covered with angular fragments of a dark brown dolerite, among which stood many large sandstone boulders that had fallen from the cliffs above. Long prisms of dolerite, a cleavage characteristic of basalts, lay like cordwood, side by side where they had split apart. Some of the sandstone boulders were streaked with black veins that were probably of organic origin and possibly fossiliferous, a surmise supported by the lumps of coal intermixed with the broken rock. The sandstone and coal came from the sedimentary strata and from black seams that were visible on the valley walls.

In the middle of Arena Valley, a small one five miles east of Beacon, we landed on a low hill that was paved with doleritic ventifacts, polished and grooved, and colored by reddish desert varnish. A thirty-knot wind made photography very difficult, but we stayed about an hour while everyone collected souvenirs.

It was now New Year's Eve. A large crowd that gathered at the Officers' Club for a celebration consumed altogether sixty cases of beer. The empty cans, stacked beside the bar in a huge pyramid, finally came down with a splendid crash. At midnight, to usher in the New Year, three thousand pounds of dynamite were to be exploded on the ice of McMurdo Sound. The intercom gave a five-second countdown, and at zero came the flash, followed instantly by a billowing black cloud, then a jolting shock, and a few seconds later the rumbling report. The black cloud drifted slowly north in the light wind, and a large black-rimmed crater marked the spot until the ice moved out some days later.

January 1, a holiday with no flying, was maddeningly bright and windless. On the second day of 1976, with a low cloud ceiling over the dry valleys, I was flown out to the edge of the dirty ice to photograph emperor penguins and killer whales. On the third day I made another visit to the Scott and Shackleton huts. I had almost run out of helicopter time, and had been saving what was left for a flight to the area around Cocks Mountain at the southern end of the Royal Society Range. I was fortunate, meanwhile, in being able to join a group of geologists on their trip to lower Taylor Valley, where I spent most of the day on Nussbaum Riegel and at Mummy Pond—my last excursion to the dry valleys.

At last the weather over the Royal Society Range improved enough to allow a flight to Cocks Mountain, scheduled for January 8. Joining me that day were Dr. Barkov, the Russian scientist, who was to be left off on Brown Peninsula, and a New Zealander with provisions for a Kiwi camp not far from Mt. Cocks. The camp consisted of a group of pyramidal red tents, each with skis and poles stuck in the snow beside it. Sledges stood on end near by, and a dog team was chained not far away. One of the New Zealanders who came crowding around to unload the crates of provisions and to talk with us told me that I should visit Ant Hill, a nunatak near Cocks Mountain where beautiful examples of sharply folded marbleized limestone could be seen. Three of the New Zealanders eagerly accepted my invitation to fly there with us, filling the Huey to capacity.

Flying south over a white, featureless, ever-widening plain, out of which the Koettlitz Glacier originates, we passed a chain of ridges and peaks buried to their tops in snow, which come to an end at a higher mountain on which much bare rock is exposed. This is Mt. Cocks. To the east of it, a group of hills rise above the snow to form a barrier, dividing the ice that flows into the Koettlitz Glacier from a tributary of another stream of ice, the huge Skelton Glacier. Along this divide, one of the nunataks could be distinguished by its truncated pyramidal shape. This was Ant Hill, our intended destination. One side is sliced away to produce a perpendicular wall on which the swirling patterns of metamorphosed limestone are plainly visible. After twice circling the hill, we flew over it to reconnoiter for a landing which was made with ease. Under patches and pockets of snow that had accumulated here and there, the convoluted gray was veined and banded by a brown-stained softer rock, broken pieces of which littered the surface. This marbleized limestone, laid down in ancient seas, was composed of the myriad skeletons of tiny marine animals. Covered by countless other sediments deposited over millions of years, it became deeply buried in the earth's crust where its character had been transformed by enormous geotectonic forces.

We returned to McMurdo late in the afternoon by way of the Kiwi camp and the Koettlitz Glacier.

FROM MONASTERY NUNATAK, A MOUNTAIN PEAK PROJECTING THROUGH THE POLAR ICE CAP

NUSSBAUM RIEGEL, A GLACIATED RIDGE AT THE FLOOR OF TAYLOR VALLEY

AIRDEVRONSIX ICEFALLS

BEACON VALLEY

BULL PASS, OLYMPUS RANGE

TRANSANTARCTIC MOUNTAINS, ON THE FLIGHT TO THE SOUTH POLE

James Clark Ross and his party, exploring farther south than anyone before, in January 1840 became the first human beings to approach this massive range. Hoping to plant the Union Jack—at the South Magnetic Pole, a point that would not be reached until 1909 by T. W. E. David and other members of a Shackleton expedition—what they found instead was this mountain barrier, flanked by a cliff of ice and guarded by two volcanic cones, which were named Erebus *and* Terror *in honor of the ships that carried his expedition.*

NUNATAKS, POLAR PLATEAU, NEAR THE SOUTH POLE

NIGHT SUN, ROSS SEA

Captain James Ross, the discoverer of the sea that bears his name, had behind him seventeen years in the Arctic when he led the first of a series of expeditions into the Antarctic towards the end of 1839. In choosing the route he took, he followed the lead of seal hunters. Having listened to their accounts of "a lagoon-like expanse of open water" beyond the ice pack within the Antarctic circle, he came prepared to enter it, in the hope of reaching the South Magnetic Pole. His ships were equipped with specially strengthened hulls for withstanding the ice. As a result, and thanks to his accomplished seamanship, they were able to pass through the consolidated ice pack and to survive the battering of a violent storm that damaged both vessels. Breaking free of the ice, they entered open water on the morning of January 9, 1840—the first men to do so—and soon came in sight of the Antarctic continent.

PACK ICE AND ICEBERG, AMUNDSEN SEA

Roald Amundsen, for whom this sea is named, organized an expedition to the South Pole that was a model of planning and efficiency. After planting the Norwegian flag in the snow at that forbidding and lonely spot where no one had ever stood before, in December 1911, a month ahead of Robert Falcon Scott's ill-fated party, they returned to their base on the Ross Ice Shelf, in perfect health, on January 25. Amundsen wrote afterward: "The great differences between Scott's expedition and mine lay in our choice of draught animals. Scott had come to the conclusion that Manchurian ponies would be superior to dogs as a means of transport. I don't suppose I was the only one to be amazed at this! For it seemed to me that conditions on the Antarctic ice-cap were precisely what one would desire for sledging with dogs. There must, I told myself, be a basic misunderstanding in the British attitude. Perhaps the dog didn't comprehend its master—or was it that the master didn't comprehend his dog?"

ICEBERG, ROSS SEA

It was near here that Ross's expedition sighted land. Robert McCormick, ship's doctor for the Erebus, recorded the following entry in his diary:

"Monday, January 11th. At 2.30 A.M. land was reported from the crow's nest. . . . It appeared at first indistinctly, through haze and a few light clouds, skirting the horizon on the port bow. . . . The whole of the upper part of this vast mountain range appeared to be a glaciation, relieved at intervals by the apex of some dark hummock or peak. . . . We had discovered a new land of so extensive a coastline and attaining such altitude as to justify the appellation of a Great New Southern Continent."

VIII. ABOARD THE ICEBREAKER *GLACIER*

The Coast Guard cutter *Glacier* had been working her way southward as she cleared a channel through McMurdo Sound for the supply ship and oil tanker that were expected to make their annual visit before the end of January. While I was stationbound by the bad weather, the Coast Guard commander at McMurdo arranged for me to be flown out to the *Glacier* to watch the icebreaking. I spent the afternoon watching from the foredeck, had supper in the wardroom, and was flown back to the station in the evening.

Three techniques are used for icebreaking: "scarfing," which consists of cutting into the ice at an angle to pry slabs off from the edge; "herringboning," which involves ramming the ice in alternating parallel tracks so as to break out a strip between; and "railroad-tracking," in which two icebreakers ram the ice along parallel courses. Herringboning was the technique I witnessed. In McMurdo Sound, the ice thus loosened is carried away on the tide or blown north by the prevailing winds.

The hull of an icebreaker has steel bow plates an inch and a half thick, and a forefoot, where the keel and stem meet, that curves up in such a way as to cause the hull to override the ice on impact. The weight and downward pressure of the ship then break off the ice. When the ice is so heavy that the ship becomes stuck and cannot back away, it can often be rolled free by rapidly pumping fuel from the tanks on one side of the ship to those on the other.

After each attack, as the ship backs away and the broken ice is churned up by the backwash from the screws, many pieces are overturned, exposing snow-free undersides tinged green and yellow-brown by algae and diatoms. Skuas, always alert for a new source of food, are thus attracted in large numbers to the wake of an icebreaker. Scarcely has the ship begun to back away before they come swarming down to pick off the organisms attached to the stained under-surfaces. So bold and greedy are they that they go right on feeding as the vessel returns to ram the ice, even as the bow seemed about to override them.

On the afternoon of January 15 I boarded the *Glacier* along with a research group headed by Dr. Theodore Foster of the Scripps Institution of Oceanography. When we sailed, at ten in the evening, the white mass of Mt. Erebus, its mantle of snow streaked gray with outcrops of bare rock, could be made out faintly in the clear eastern sky. A pennant of smoke and condensed vapors, ethereal yet unchanging, floated north from the crater.

The next morning the ship was sixty miles northeast of Ross Island. Mt. Erebus and Mt. Terror, its twin volcanoes were still in sight on the southern horizon. This was to be my last view of Antarctica for ten days, during a 2,300-mile voyage through the Ross, the Amundsen, and the Bellingshausen seas to Palmer Station, and from there to the Weddell Sea, where Dr. Foster and his party were to carry on their research. As we steamed northward, the ice floes became more extensive and reached to the horizon on both sides. As the ice became thicker, we crashed unavoidably into some of these, splitting them and driving the fragments apart. Each time we hit the ice, the blow would throw the ship to one side. The sensation was much like that of driving over a rutted road in a truck with stiff springs. Icebraking is accompanied by thumping and scraping sounds against and along the hull, and by the sloshing of the broken pieces as the bow wave overturns them.

In the afternoon the ship's helicopters were dispatched on reconnaissance flights, and I went along to take photographs. The flight lasted for two hours and took us somewhere between sixty and eighty miles ahead of the ship. Scattered floes of snow-covered pack ice varying in extent from acres to a few yards across, smooth white on top, their icy borders tinted pale blue and green, lay in a dark, steely sea flecked with whitecaps and small cakes of ice. For an observer from the air, all sense of scale disappears, and it becomes impossible to guess the true size of unidentified objects beneath. As we flew at from 1,500 to 2,000 feet, we saw occasional seals, mere specks on the white surface. At five hundred feet, the few Adélie penguins we saw could be easily distinguished as they raced away in panic from the sound of the machine.

Thirty miles away from the *Glacier*, we encountered a foglike layer of low cloud at five hundred feet, well below the high overcast. Taking altitude, we flew ahead, looking meanwhile for openings in the gray floor of banded clouds through which we could descend for a view of the sea and ice. The helicopters kept in constant communication and stayed within sight of one another whenever possible. When the decision was made to descend through the cloud cover, the helos took separate directions so as to minimize the chance of collision. The descent was an abrupt severing of all connection with the physical world, to enter a gray, dimensionless nonworld in which the concept of distance meant nothing. When we broke through the low clouds, at six hundred feet above the sea, the first thing we saw was the faint outline of an ice edge against the darker gray of water; the snow surface itself was undifferentiated from the surrounding fog. To me the ice here looked no different from the ice that had surrounded the *Glacier* when we took off. We rose above the fog and turned back towards the ship, both helos flying along together. Once we had left the low clouds behind, we descended again to six hundred feet; whenever seals were spotted, the helicopter circled low so that I could photograph them. Except for one leopard seal, they were all of the Weddell species. With the door open, wearing the required rubber dry suit, I had become very cold and was glad to see the icebreaker again, plowing slowly along so far below that it could have been a plaything.

On the horizon, in every direction, tabular icebergs were to be seen, although few were close to the ship's course. Some of the floes were very hummocky, the blocks of ice heaped in wild disorder. These were probably the remains of pressure ridges produced during the winter. Where they occurred, and also on the sheer sides of icebergs, blue ice showed through the cover of snow. The blue ice in bergs is denser and older than the sea ice of the floes, which becomes mushy during the summer and is easily broken. In fact, sea ice generally appears to be made up of poorly consolidated snow. Yellowish, decaying, ice extends out from the edge of the floes to form an underwater shelf, and curling over the edge of this submerged layer is a white crust of snow perhaps two feet thick. When the ship's wake hits, this white upper layer breaks off in long strips that rapidly crumble and disintegrate in the water.

In the days that followed, with no difference from one to the next and no alternation between light and darkness, heavy clouds hung low over floes of broken ice that rested immobile on an iron-gray sea. Icebergs were all about, both the tabular bergs that originate in the ice shelf and those with pointed and lofty tops that are calved from glaciers. We continued to push northeast, trying to conserve fuel so that more would be available for Dr. Foster's work in the Weddell Sea. To take the shortest course would mean battling thick pack ice, a slow process and wasteful of fuel; the way around the ice to the north, on the other hand, was so much longer as to make any real saving of fuel unlikely. So a compromise between the two routes was sought. During the second night, however, the ice became so thick that the ship had to backtrack in search of open leads. The next morning the ice was still very heavy, but open water was beginning to show towards the north—although estimating ice conditions from shipboard is difficult because the ice always appears denser on the horizon than it does close to the ship.

We kept to a northeasterly course of 40 by the compass under a perennially gray sky. Except that a twenty-knot wind arose out of the east and kicked up whitecaps in the widest leads, the weather was unchanged. Crossing the International Date Line at Longitude 180° on this easterly course, we had two Mondays in succession. On the following night the sea ice became much reduced, and just north of Latitude 68°S our course was changed first to 90 and then to 100, which was approximately a Great Circle course for Anvers Island. The dense pack ice that made the continent so inaccessible to sailing ships was at last well to the south. But the gloomy weather continued; as the monotonous gray clouds closed in, visibility was reduced, with a prospect of fog. A long slow swell became perceptible—the seas of the stormy fifties had been damped down by sea ice below the Antarctic Convergence. Gradually the condition of the ice changed, from compact discrete floes to brash—a mixture of small fragments and slush—and isolated cakes. Small rectangular icebergs, dingy gray in the subdued light, rode the horizon to port and starboard. Meanwhile, the wind moderated and shifted to the southeast.

On January 19 the *Glacier* was 970 miles from McMurdo but still more than 1,500 miles west of the Antarctic Peninsula. White ice islands with blue-green translucent margins stood out in sharp contrast with the gray of sea and sky in this changeless Antarctic scene, where the only visible living things were pelagic birds—the buff-winged Antarctic petrel and the snow petrel, that pure white, illusive wraith of the southernmost icebound seas. In these cold waters the petrels obtain a living from an unsuspected richness of marine life. They flew past the ship singly or in small groups, evidently out of curiosity, twisting and turning in the wind, dipping and rising with the air currents.

In the afternoon the wind stiffened to twenty knots. Poor visibility obscured the icebergs a few miles off; closer ones stood out white against the black water, and the Prussian blue of the deeper recesses of the small icebergs (known as growlers) from which the snow had been washed away, added to the sense of an inhospitable cold. The fog thickened as the afternoon advanced. The course of the *Glacier*, now at 110, was taking her back again towards the continent and closer to the pack ice. We were sighting larger floes and encountering more icebergs. Gradually the pack and brash ice became so thick that the ship began plowing through them, producing all the sounds of hard ice striking against her hull. The next morning the sky brightened but the fog persisted, approaching whiteout conditions because of the fine ice crystals in the air. In all directions brash and cakes of ice uniformly covered the sea. A swell ran through the pack, raising and lowering it in long, slow undulations.

By ten that night the clouds in the southern sky had thinned and the sun, a fuzzy white globe, shone low over the horizon. The sky above it was streaked with pale pink stratocirrus clouds, and below lay a bank of fog darker than the sea. A reflection of the sun's faint disc, surrounded by a halo of amber light that faded outward to many times its diameter, was caught between the rafts of ice in the ruffled sea. About fifteen degrees to the left of the sun and at the same altitude a prismatic display, a refractive atmospheric phenomenon, appeared linked to a small spurious sun that was leashed by a golden band to the orb itself.

After the evening meal on January 21, we learned that an engine-room petty officer had been electrocuted when he accidentally touched an open high-voltage circuit, and that the course of the *Glacier* had been reversed so that the seaman's body could be transferred to the *Burton Island* in McMurdo Sound, for a flight back to the United States. The effect of all this was to delay our arrival at Palmer Station by at least six days.

Snow fell during the night, blanketing the ship, and continued to fall in the morning, whipped by a strong east wind. We were running through patches of dense pack ice separated by open stretches of water.

Crabeater seals, recognizable by their light color and doglike muzzles, were much more numerous than on the outward trip. As the ship approached a sleeping seal, the animal would raise its head to stare in bewilderment at the monstrous object bearing down on it, waiting until the last minute to plunge into the water. Adélie penguins stood on the ice pans in groups of a dozen or more, curiously watching our approach and then hurrying away as the ship loomed over them. Snow petrels were abundant and for the first time I saw Arctic terns; indistinguishable in breeding plumage from the Antarctic species, their black bills identified these as wintering birds from the northern hemisphere. All day we drove through an ice-covered sea under a white sky. From below deck, ice scraping along the hull sounded like surf on a gravel beach.

When I awoke in the morning and realized that the ship was not moving, I thought we had reached our rendezvous point. It turned out, however, that we were beset in a polynya—a body of water surrounded by pack ice—and still 390 miles from the meeting place. The ice surface was very irregular. Smooth, snow-covered areas were fenced in by ridges composed of upended blocks, and by hillocks of ice that had built up to a considerable height, an indication of recent extreme lateral pressures. Icebergs frozen into the pack ice that surrounded the small pond where the ship was trapped were everywhere—large and small, some flat-topped and others with bizarrely shaped, jagged peaks. Extending around three-quarters of the horizon, a narrow yellow band cast a brighter light on the distant bergs, indicating that clearer skies were not far away. . Whenever a peak of ice was momentarily struck by a shaft of sunlight, it would light up as though illuminated from within.

A helicopter was launched so that the executive officer could reconnoiter the ice pack. The officer was then able to guide the ship through an escape route he had discovered. He described the situation as like being lost in a maze; the way out could be found only from above.

The next morning the *Glacier* was again dead in the water, but this time we had reached the designated meeting place within sight of Erebus and Terror—a view that ten days before I had expected never to see again. The sea was glassy and the sky cloudless. Since the *Burton Island* had not left McMurdo to meet us, our helicopters were dispatched to the station with the body of the seaman. As soon as they returned we got under way again for Palmer Station.

The weather was much improved, sunny and warmer with a light southerly breeze that had cleared away the ice. But by evening we had again entered heavy pack. The unit for measuring the density of pack ice is an octa—that is, an eighth of a square mile. A rating of eight octas would mean that the sea was completely covered with pack, and four octas would mean it was half covered. The density of the ice, estimated at four or five octas, increased until the ship was threading narrow winding leads. The weather remained fair, however, the pleasantest it had been since we first left McMurdo on January 16. The following day was brilliant, with ice floes and icebergs on all sides, and the condition of the ice pack was down to one or two octas. The colors were more varied than on any day so far. The reflection of the low sun in the small waves was so dazzling that I could not look at it directly. The wrinkled dark blue of the sea was streaked horizontally with darker facets and speckled with pieces of ice and occasional breaking wavelets. Icebergs, mostly tabular, rose black against the sun, whereas those facing it in the opposite quarter were a glaring white. The snow cover on the floes and on the sloping sides of the icebergs was tinted a lavender pink; hollows in the snow and under the ice blocks on old pressure ridges were a deep ultramarine blue; and where the underwater extensions of the floes were washed by waves, they were a pale blue-green.

Good days are the exception in the seas that surround the Antarctic Continent, and one rarely followed another. It was no surprise, therefore, when low gray clouds returned with a near-zero ceiling, intermittently reducing visibility to a few hundred yards. Now and again for a tantalizing moment the clouds would disperse to reveal a pallid northern sun.

The condition of the ice was extremely variable. For a while the sea was covered by smooth-topped polygonal rafts of decaying sea ice, separated into floes by a network of narrow channels of open water. Many seals—crabeaters, Weddells, and a few leopard seals—lay on the larger floes, and from time to time groups of Adélie and emperor penguins riding on smaller floes slid past the ship. A hazy sun, shining momentarily through a break in the clouds, cast a yellow tint on the metallic ocean surface between the pans of ice.

Later that day we left the ice behind, traveling for many miles through an ice-free sea. But then we came to more sea ice—circular pans that had the shape of enormous lily pads with turned-up margins—and after that we began encountering still larger cakes, with brash filling much of the space between. On open stretches with a sheen like pewter, new ice was forming in thin brittle plates, advancing in curved bands that became a shield against the wind, in much the way that oil smooths the surface of water. Moved by a cross swell undulating at random, the surface constantly changed, looking now like metal, then like silk. Icebergs were always in view.

A low gray overcast can give a clue to the condition of sea ice in the distance. Over open water the cloud cover shades from pearly gray high up, where light from above penetrates directly, to a dark band on the horizon where it touches the sea and where the slanting rays of light reach the observer through a greater thickness of cloud. When, however, pack ice covers the sea beyond the horizon, most of the sunlight that filters down is reflected back by the white surface, illuminating the clouds from below. Then a white band—called an ice blink—replaces the dark one along the horizon. Sometimes these effects are seen in juxtaposition, where an ice floe beyond the horizon ends and the ice blink is abruptly replaced by a dark strip. Where the clouds are very low and the sea is completely covered with pack ice, the reflection from the surface can produce a whiteout, in which light, direct and reflected, is scattered by ice crystals in the air.

By January 30 we had regained the distance lost in retracing our course, but we were still more than 1500 miles from Palmer Station. Cruising along in the Amundsen Sea, two hundred miles from the coast of Marie Byrd Land, we were north of the dense sea ice, and encountered only loose pack and intermittent patches of brash. Icebergs, however, continued to be numerous. The temperature was well below freezing and ice formed on the lee side of ice rafts where the water was unruffled. Certainly the freezing I observed did not presage the advent of winter; rather, it was a transitory phenomenon which could take place at any time during the summer when the temperature drops below freezing. Sea water does not begin to freeze in earnest until March.

Occasionally we passed close to an iceberg and could see, underneath the breaking waves, the blue of its submerged foundations. The great majority of bergs are white, but once in a while we would see one composed of the older, harder ice that was entirely and intensely blue, not simply below the water or in its wave-eroded caverns. The blueness of pure dense ice is said to be due to dissolved air under pressure; when pieces are placed in water, that air escapes with a crackling sound.

The heavy overcast stayed with us into the early days of February, and fog was not only an imminent possibility but also a frequent presence. Visibility could suddenly decrease to a quarter of a mile or less as the ship entered a bank of sea fog, and then as quickly increase when the ship emerged. In this tenebrous atmosphere, where objects were not sharply defined, any judgment of distance or size was uncertain. Icebergs that had been thought to be far off would loom up, unexpectedly close; others would turn out to be more distant than had been supposed. The officers on the bridge kept careful watch for icebergs by radar. On February 3 the ship's position was 68° 49′ S latitude and 102° W longitude, 970 miles from Palmer Station. The nearest land was Cape Peterson, more than two hundred miles due south. At this latitude and time of year the sun set briefly. Darkness was never complete, but the twilight was often greatly prolonged by fog.

During the night of February 4 we passed fifty miles north of Peter I Island, named for the Russian Tsar by Bellingshausen. Peter I Island has rarely been seen and seldom visited. Shrouded in fog and encircled by icebergs and impenetrable ice pack, the island is unapproachable from the sea. Reputedly a home for penguins and Antarctic seals, the twelve-mile-long islet lies in the Bellingshausen Sea, 270 miles north of the uncharted and unmapped Eights Coast of Antarctica and more than four hundred miles west of Palmer Land on the Antarctic Peninsula.

The executive officer had offered the day before to have the helicopters fly me and another passenger to Peter I Island to see and photograph it and, weather permitting, to land. We took off in the morning, heading south by west towards the island which was now astern sixty miles away. After we had flown about twenty miles the sea became obscured by clouds, which continued to thicken until the pilot decided that a view of the island would be unlikely and to land impossible; so we turned back towards the *Glacier*. By way of consolation, the helicopters circled for an hour over the ice floes so that we could photograph and make a count of seals. We saw a great number of all three common species of seal—and, according to my fellow passenger, one rare Ross Seal as well. That there were so many seals hinted at a very large population around Peter I Island.

The *Glacier* continued her eastward course that day and the next. During that time, floating ice thinned out and finally disappeared altogether. The wind increased steadily from the northeast, until we were bucking a forty-knot gale and the sea was white with breaking waves. The ship pitched sluggishly into the onrushing seas, throwing spray high over the bow and the superstructure of the bridge. Low stratus clouds added to the stormy scene. My only solace was the birds that had increased greatly in number and in kind as we neared the Antarctic Peninsula. Flocks of cape pigeons flew past, wheeling and gliding in the troughs of waves; albatrosses appeared, both the gray-headed and the wandering species, and many southern fulmars in their rather nondescript, dirty-gray plumage.

One day a flock of ten or fifteen Antarctic petrels fed on the sea beside the ship, fluttering and snatching food from the surface. Sometimes they alighted on the water and dived immediately, emerging a moment later. The flock moved along while feeding, as though they might be following a school of krill. I also saw larger flocks, containing many hundreds of birds that milled about over the ice floes on which other petrels were resting, in such great number that when they all took flight together, presenting their white underplumage to view, they became a filmy cloud, evanescent as a puff of snow.

IX. LAST DAYS AT PALMER STATION

We had expected to arrive at Palmer Station late on February 6, but because of fog, which obscured the intricate approaches to Arthur Harbor on Anvers Island, the *Glacier* was hove to until daylight. As she proceeded to anchorage the next morning, I was flown to the station with all my baggage. To enable me to get pictures from the air the helicopter pilot circled over the station and the nearby islands.

From under the crumbling front of the massive Marr Ice Piedmont glacier, which extends back and upward from the shore for many miles to the foot of Mt. Francais, small tongues of gray rock project into the sea. Viewed from over a thousand feet up, the buildings of the research station that cling to these barren scraps of land appeared like ant hills in a cracked pavement. Next to the enormous ice sheet, even the security and permanence of the rock on which the station was built seemed uncertain—as though the balance of forces could as easily tilt in favor of an advance as of a retreat by the ice sheet.

When I arrived at Palmer the *Hero* was in Ushuaia on Tierra del Fuego and was not expected back until the third week of February. This meant I had time for a visit to the islands near the station.

Black clouds obscured the mountains of the peninsula to the southeast for most of my first day, but from time to time they lifted to give brief views through a slot on the horizon of pink sunlit peaks. The bad weather continued the following day. On February 9, however, a break in the heavy overcast accompanied by moderating winds gave promise of brighter conditions. After the midday meal, Bill Fraser and I took a Zodiac to Bonaparte Point, which is separated from the Palmer Station peninsula by a long narrow inlet. Fraser, a University of Minnesota ornithologist, has been observing the gull colony of Bonaparte Point since egg-laying began in December. He hoped on this day to round up all the unfledged, banded chicks for measuring and weighing.

Bonaparte Point is a narrow neck of glacier-scoured, deeply gullied gray granite on which blocks torn from their original attachments by past glaciation lie scattered about. In crevices and hollows, tufts of grass and moss have taken root over the years, fertilized by bird excrement and the decayed remains of organisms gathered from the sea by the gulls. A favorite food of the black-backed gulls is limpets; the flat conical shells of these mollusks, measuring from one to two inches across, filled the spaces between the fragmented rocks in places where the gulls had established feeding stations.

Shortly after we landed the clouds settled down again and snow began to fall. It went on falling throughout the afternoon. I passed the time exploring the peninsula while Fraser pursued the agile and elusive gull chicks, some of which escaped by taking to the water. On a small enclosed rocky beach I came across a crabeater seal whose lethargic response to my inquisitiveness was in striking contrast to the panic of the young gulls.

During the days that followed, whenever the weather was good and the wind less than fifteen knots—the limit for going out in a Zodiac—I went with Bill Fraser to the islands that surround Arthur Harbor. The most distant of these was Cormorant Island, three miles to the southeast, and the nearest was Torgerson, a half mile from the station on the west of the harbor. Bill's work with skuas and gulls, and to a limited degree with giant petrels, entailed frequent followup visits. My presence at the station helped him because of the strict rule that no one may venture forth in a Zodiac alone.

On stormy days, I would walk the few hundred yards to the foot of the glacier behind the station to observe the working of the forces that held sea, land, and ice in their dubious equilibrium. The surging waves washed incessantly over rounded gray blocks of granite, slippery with algae, and growled in the towering wall of ice they were continually undermining. Chunks of ice broke away from the horizontal slots melted by the sea into the foot of the glacier, to produce a slushy brash which the waves beating against the rocks rapidly disintegrated. To suppose that the sea was gaining in its contest with the ice would be to ignore the vast reserve within the Anvers Island Glacier, ever pressing forward from the land behind, and the fact that on the rocky spit where I stood the cliff of ice was firmly fixed. From the corner formed by the junction of sea, ice, and land, the glacier front curved away to a cove enclosed in ice. The cliff became ragged with fissures; slabs and small bergs were continually spalling off with an explosive noise followed by a splashing roar.

Sometimes on bad days I would cross over to Bonaparte Point by means of a cableway that bridged the inlet. A boatswain's chair suspended from a trolley rode the single cable. You shoved off from either side and sped away on a catenary course to the low point of the cable, pulling yourself the rest of the way from there with a line attached to the cable supports on either side of the inlet. To climb into the tippy seat with camera and tripod required considerable dexterity, especially as the trolley had a tendency to start off before you were ready. Unless you made the trip empty-handed it was advisable to get help for the launching; otherwise you could find yourself suspended embarrassingly over the middle of the channel, unable to pull back to shore because of having lost your hold on the line.

The atmospheric conditions over Anvers Island, which so often had a way of confirming my suspicion about the malignity of inanimate nature, appeared to be locally generated, for frequently when the weather was bad at the station, with snow flurries and lowering clouds, there would be a light band around the horizon, indicating sunshine everywhere else. Often at these times the mountains of the peninsula and the ice cap to the southeast could be seen, yellow in the sun, through this slot under the clouds.

If by noon the stalled weather had dissipated or drifted north, Bill would suggest a trip to one of the islands and we would carry outboard motors, gasoline cans, life jackets, walkie-talkies, and oars down to the dock where the Zodiacs were launched by means of a hand-operated crane. Safety regulations required that life jackets always be worn on boat trips and that the equipment include a spare motor, oars, and a radio. Before departing we had to call the station's radio operator to let him know our destination and the approximate length of our excursion. This information was written on a blackboard in the common room. We were also required to call the station operator on arrival at our destination and to keep him informed of our plans.

On one of these afternoons Bill and I took a Zodiac to Litchfield Island,* where fur seals had been seen by another research team the day before. On the beach where landings were customarily made, several Weddell seals were basking on the shingle above the high-tide mark. They paid little attention to us until we walked right up to them. Then they began anxiously squirming backwards. But lethargy soon overtook them again and they had to be goaded into raising their heads to stare at us out of watery, myopic eyes. On my first visit to Litchfield the year before, a herd of elephant seals in various stages of molt had occupied the left-hand rocky abutment to the beach. On this day there were no elephant seals. Above the gravel, however, among the gray lichened rocks and mosses we spotted a bull fur seal. He was well camouflaged and we might have overlooked him had he not taken alarm.

*Now a Specially Protected Area under the Antarctic Treaty and off limits to all but scientists with a pressing need to visit it.

Fur seals belong to a different family within the order *Pinnipedia* from all the other seals found in Antarctica. Like the sea lions, with which they have close affinities, they have external ears (hence the term eared seals) and hind limbs that can be folded forward under their bodies so as to be used for locomotion on land. Neither of these traits is shared by the true seals, which have traveled further along the course of evolution away from their terrestrial ancestors than the fur seals. The structure of their hind limbs and the size of their fore limbs give the fur seals a posture more erect than that of the true seals, and they are more agile on land. This difference was quickly evident to us when we tried to photograph the bull fur seal close up; he scrambled over the rocks with great ease and we had a lively time getting pictures of him. Fur seals are far less tolerant of man than the true seals, and with good reason.

From the top of the beach the land leveled off to form a narrow valley whose floor sloped gradually for about a quarter of a mile to a shallow cove enclosed by bare rocky hills. This was a muddy place where elephant seals liked to wallow. On the day of our visit we found only the wide, grooved tracks that showed they had recently been there. The tide was out, so that we could walk all the way across the head of the cove to its far shore where the mud bottom gave way to a pavement of small, surf-polished boulders. A compacted snowbank covered the shore on one side of the valley's extension; its edge, undermined by the sea at high tide, was tinted red by a growth of algae. Icy chunks of snow, stranded by the retreating tide, lay in the mud below the bank from which they had fallen. On the far side of the cove, beyond the polished boulders, we came upon the elephant seals huddled together, their sloughing coats all in tatters. They responded to our intrusion by threateningly rearing up and gaping at us.

Since Palmer Station is north of the Antarctic Circle, the sun sets in summer for a few hours every night; at midnight in midsummer it drops below the horizon for about an hour of twilight. During my stay in February the nights were getting longer, and there were short periods of complete darkness. At this high latitude the sun's position was at an angle so low that its course was almost parallel to the horizon. Sunset displays and twilight were both greatly prolonged. It was when the sky was streaked with high, thin clouds that the most spectacular sunsets would occur, the colors slowly intensifying from pale yellow and pink to deep orange and russet against a light blue background that shaded off into apple green. The effect might last for an hour; as the light faded, the fiery display slowly darkened and became diffused into the purple of the night sky. Equally dramatic were the colors produced by the setting sun, just before it disappeared below the horizon, on Anvers Glacier, across the harbor. Where its rays lit the ice cliffs directly, they turned a sulphur yellow that burnished the sea below them in paths of gold. Cakes of ice floating in the harbor, miniatures of the parent ice sheet, picked up the same color where they faced the sun. On these surfaces that were illuminated at an angle, the colors were pinkish mauve, lilac, and lavender. In shadow, they were dark purple and blue.

Humble Island, north of Litchfield and about the same distance from Palmer Station, is noted for an Adélie rookery and a colony of giant petrels, along with the ubiquitous skuas that are found wherever there are other birds to prey upon, and also a herd of elephant seals. Still another feature is a fresh-water pond fed by melting snow, a stercoraceous mudhole that is occupied from time to time by the elephant seals. The giant petrels—also, and more correctly, known as southern giant fulmars—successfully hold their own against predation by the skuas. On the day of my visit with Bill Fraser, the adults were guarding fat downy chicks and were hard to displace in order to weigh and band their young. Handling the adults was tricky because of the oily, persistently foul-smelling liquid they regurgicate—whether as a defensive action or not is unclear. At one nest both adults were in attendance—the female presumably guarding the chick, her mate standing close by. At too close an approach or too sudden a move the male would spread his wings in what seemed a protective gesture while the female jabbed in my direction—whereupon I would back off rather than provoke further reaction.

The skuas here were the most aggressive of this species I had ever encountered. The adult birds launched a fierce diving attack, not hesitating to strike me, so that I felt obliged to hold my tripod high above my head for protection. The unfledged gray chicks wandering among the gray rocks were so well camouflaged that I had come upon them quite by accident. The adults' attacks, accompanied by chattering cries, continued unrelenting so long as I remained within fifty feet of the young birds, and since several pairs of skuas had chicks in the same general region, I was under attack no matter where I turned. Weary of trying to fend off this tireless divebombing, which might come from any direction, I left for another part of the island.

The place of greatest interest on Humble Island was the Adélie penguin rookery. Most of the chicks here were shedding, sloughing off gray baby down in patches that gave them a motheaten look. Tufts of down clung to the developing juvenile plumage that had pushed through from beneath, and some young penguins, newly clad in flawless black and white feathers, still wore capes of fluff that made them look hunchbacked and elderly. One particularly amusing young bird still wore a patch of down on the top of his head like a Tam O'Shanter. The rookery was almost completely deserted by the adults, who were away foraging for themselves and their hungry offspring. In such a community of juveniles, gathered in dense throngs that effectively wiped out all territorial boundaries, a question arose: Did the returning parents recognize their own young, or did they simply feed those that most vigorously importuned them? There was evidence to support both hypotheses. An adult from the sea was immediately approached by several young birds, some of which might have been her own. They pecked at her throat and bill to provoke the feeding response. However, the first reaction of the old bird was usually a series of retaliatory jabbings and evasions. As she fled she would be pursued by one or two chicks; this seemed to stimulate her to even more rapid flight, and a race was on. An adult penguin, closely followed by two full-grown downy youngsters, running through the rookery and dodging about in an apparent attempt to shake them off, was a common sight. Unexpectedly, with what appeared to be a resigned desperation, the adult would turn around, feed one of her pursuers by regurgitation, and then dash off again at once. The pursuit would continue until both young birds had been satisfied. Was this possibly a strategy by which parents were able to separate their own young from the crowd and thus assure that they were not feeding impostors?

During the summer months, ships of various national registries not infrequently call at Palmer Station. They come on missions of science and exploration, adventure and tourism. The scientific ships are mostly from England, Chile, and Argentina, the three nations whose territorial claims on the peninsula have been put in abeyance for the duration of the Antarctic Treaty.

Late in the evening of February 12 one of the most famous of these ships, the *Lindblad Explorer*, steamed into Arthur Harbor under an orange sunset sky. The next morning, according to the custom at Palmer Station, an open house for the passengers and members of the crew was declared—although a few laboratories remained closed to visitors because of crucial experiments in progress. In return for the station's hospitality, the residents of the station were invited on board the *Explorer* for cocktails and lunch.

The next morning, another beautiful day for which Bill Fraser and I had planned a trip to Cormorant Island, it was announced at breakfast that Italian mountaineers had arrived in a chartered Norwegian oilrig tender and would be entertained at the station. They stayed only a few hours, and left before lunch. In the afternoon, Bill and I made our expedition to Cormorant Island by Zodiac, weaving our way through much floating ice. Near our landing place, an ice cake no more than twenty feet across held a crowd of at least sixteen crabeater seals. Still other seals were continually shooting up onto it from the water, and those on board were as regularly slipping off. While Fraser headed for the island's interior in search of his banded skuas, I revisited the Adélie colony where I had taken photographs the year before. As on Humble Island, the birds were mostly molting juveniles, huddled into one rather small area with only a few adults among them. A nearby promontory, which not long before had been the center of an active population, was now without birds. All around and over the pearly gray, smoothly rounded stones was a litter of mud, molted feathers, and refuse from the once thriving colony. Coating the stones was a natural gesso composed of bird lime and other organic substances that had been polished by the rubbing of countless Adélie bodies.

Cormorant Island lies about half a mile from the south shore of Anvers Island, in view of the Anvers Island glacier where it terminates in an unstable cliff fifty or more feet high. Continuously adjusting to the seaward movement of the ice sheet, the glacier kept up a constant cracking and growling all afternoon. At intervals an explosive report would precede a thundering rumble as a block of ice broke loose and crashed into the sea, to be followed by an avalanche of both ice and snow. The spawning of icebergs was in progress.

On a terraced cliff rising above the cove where we landed, hundreds of blue-eyed shags were nesting. Most of the young birds were already acquiring their juvenile plumage; a few already had well-developed flight feathers, whereas some still quite small birds were in the downy stage. At each nest, with the exception of those containing well-advanced young, an adult shag was on guard. From time to time a bird would fly in from the sea, coming in low across the water and swooping up the face of the cliff to alight beside the nest where its mate was standing. The ceremony of recognition and place-changing at the nest would begin now, its posturing and nodding accompanied by guttural sounds. After this ritual, the mate just relieved would turn and glide down and away towards the sea. While the newcomer settled into place on the edge of the nest, its charges would be excitedly begging for food. After a few minutes they would be fed by regurgitation, with the young bird inserting its bill into the throat of the adult. The feeding was usually repeated several times, each young bird taking its turn. Blue-eyed cormorants do not appear to be unduly disturbed by human visitors near their nests, provided the visitors do not move about. Sudden motions, however, can provoke a protective response. I first noticed this reaction when I stood up quickly after having crouched beside a nest for some time. The parent shag facing me from the opposite side of the nest immediately spread its wings to cover the young. After a few seconds it resumed its former position, with wings folded; but every time I made a sudden move it repeated the performance.

The white, chickenlike sheathbill, the only Antarctic bird without webbed feet, is a commensal in cormorant colonies, where it scavenges decayed and regurgitated fish, the contents of broken eggs, and dead shag chicks. It is often seen pecking at the refuse around cormorant nests, where the larger birds ignore its activities. Sheathbills raise their young in close association with the cormorants on which they so largely depend for a livelihood. They lay their eggs in a hollow or under an overhanging rock, which is a protection against accidental destruction by the cormorants and a safe retreat for the precocial young. One family of sheathbills, occupying a cavity in the cliff where I had been photographing shags, consisted of two young birds, nearly full grown and soon to be fledged. Every time the adult sheathbill returned to the nest site with a scavenged morsel, these young ones would emerge to be fed; sometimes they would leave the security of their cave and run several yards to meet the parent bird. The sheathbills' dependence on shags is seasonal; when the latter have departed for the winter, they find another source of food in the marine life of the tidal littoral. The garbage dumps of the year-round research establishments* have recently become a winter bonanza for these birds. At Palmer Station, I was told, sheathbills are the commonest birds in winter, with considerable numbers of them foraging in the dump like domestic chickens.

On the way back from Cormorant Island we stopped at Hermit Island, where Bill had been working with a colony of black-backed gulls. We landed in a quiet cove, where above the stony beach a permanent bank of ice and snow, green with algae, filled a little valley for a quarter of a mile into the interior. One Weddell and two crabeater seals were stretched out on the snow near the beach. The crabeaters were indifferent to my presence but the Weddell moved away as I approached. Its hide, stained green by algae, had an unnatural look. Near the seals three Adélie penguins were alternately preening and eating snow by burrowing into it head first. The black-backed gulls had colonized a cliff overlooking one side of the valley. Here by force of numbers they were able to hold their own against the skuas that had taken possession of most of the island, and which attacked us with unabating ferocity as soon as we went inland from the shore.

A third island on which we landed, known as Shortcut, is also a breeding place for skuas. I saw no other birds here; clearly the aggressive skuas are able to preempt smaller islands for their exclusive use. Given the way birds normally colonize a new territory, beginning with a few pairs, it would not have been possible for another species to withstand the overwhelming predatory pressure of the skuas.

A unique feature of Shortcut is a thick growth of moss and lichens filling a wide trough that runs between two rock ridges and divides the island roughly in half. Underlying this bed of vegetation is a gravel substratum over which a thin layer of black organic matter has accumulated, and which is cut through by a maze of channels. Lichens form a white growth along the borders of these channels and on clumps of dead moss. The age of the moss must be considerable, in view of its extremely slow growth, retarded by a covering of snow, patches of which were still present on this February day, throughout much of the year.

Ever since my arrival at Palmer Station, a large iceberg had been grounded in the next bay south of Bonaparte Peninsula, which Bill Fraser had unofficially named Kristi Cove. At the station the iceberg was watched with interest, for the good reason that as it melted and became lighter it would eventually float free, with the likelihood that it might drift into Arthur Harbor and become an obstacle to navigation. That afternoon during our visit to Shortcut the wind stiffened, raising whitecaps. Hoping to avoid a soaking on our return trip, we ran our Zodiac in the protective lee of a small island off the entrance to Kristi Cove—a maneuver that brought us close to the stranded iceberg. On our way to Cormorant Island we had seen that it took the form of an arch, an aspect not visible from the station. We decided to have a closer look. Because of the iceberg's massive size, the opening through it had seemed small from a distance; now, on closer view, we saw that it was such that a large motorboat could easily pass through. Tempted to try it ourselves, after considering that icebergs have an unpredictable habit of turning over, we gave up the project. We did, however, go close enough to see, framed by the magnificent arc of ice, Anvers Island glacier, blue in shadow, and of Mt. Français gleaming in the late afternoon sun.

Bad weather once again enveloped Palmer Station, bringing low clouds, intermittent rain and snow, and strong winds. For two days there were no excursions to other islands. Tantalizingly, the sun shone golden from under the overcast, lighting up the mountains to the south. On the third day, although we were able to go

---

*Palmer Station seals all its garbage in 55-gallon drums and disposes of it far out at sea.

WIENCKE ISLAND, FROM BISMARCK STRAIT

WIENCKE ISLAND, FROM NEUMAYER CHANNEL

STRANDED ICEBERG, ARGENTINE ISLANDS

SCHOLLAERT CHANNEL

GREEN AND PINK ALGAE IN SNOWBANKS, ARGENTINE ISLANDS

SMITH ISLAND, FROM SCHOLLAERT CHANNEL

SCHOLLAERT CHANNEL

MOUNTAIN PEAK, NEAR BISMARCK STRAIT

EVENING LIGHT, SOUTH OF BISMARCK STRAIT

HERO, HEADING SOUTH TOWARDS MELCHIOR ISLANDS

MELCHIOR ISLANDS, BETWEEN ANVERS AND BRABANT ISLANDS

JADE ICEBERG, COLORED BY ALGAE AND PLANKTON, STRANDED OFF LIVINGSTON ISLAND

once more to Litchfield Island, before we started back the clouds had shut in again and it had begun to snow. Three more days of rain and snow followed, with strong northwest winds which gradually subsided on the third day, bringing fog.

At 10:30 in the morning of February 21, the *Hero* steamed into Arthur Harbor and tied up to the wharf. I was on the dock along with everyone else to greet her. Seeing me from the deck, Captain Lenie called out in his characteristically sardonic manner, "Hello, old man."

That afternoon, conditions had improved enough to permit Fraser and me to pay one last visit to Cormorant Island. The wind rose while we were preoccupied with the birds, and we found ourselves heading into a twenty-four-knot breeze on the return journey. As we rounded Bonaparte Point to enter the quieter waters of Arthur Harbor, a heavy surf was breaking against the rocks, throwing spray high over the point. Wet and uncomfortable, we were glad to be back.

X. ABOARD THE *HERO*

On February 22 I joined the *Hero* for a visit to the Joubin Islands, where ornithologists Everett Douglas and Russell Lockner went ashore to capture chinstrap penguins. I changed my mind about going with them after a heavy wet snow began to fall—and regretted my decision later, on hearing that they had discovered a large herd of fur seals there. By the time the *Hero* returned to base for lunch, the iceberg stranded in Kristi Cove had indeed floated free and been carried by the tide into Arthur Harbor. Considerably smaller now as a result of having turned over and partly broken apart, it was still a formidable mass of ice. During the evening the rising tide carried the iceberg inshore, uncomfortably close to the *Hero* in her berth at the pier. She was to sail at 4:00 A.M. the next day on a dredging expedition to Brabant, the island next north of Anvers, and Captain Lenie decided for the safety of the ship to cast off and anchor for the night out in the harbor. After supper I gave up my room in the station and moved on board with all my baggage.

I awoke shortly after six, dressed, and went on deck. The *Hero* was passing through Neumayer Strait—a quite different place now from my memory of it in brilliant evening sunlight. Low clouds and fog shrouded the mountains on either side. In places the lower slopes showed through the murk, and occasionally there would be a glimpse of the summits. The channel was almost ice-free, but somber and forbidding; under the heavy overcast the idyllic display of pastel colors that had so impressed me a year ago were not to be seen. Emerging into Gerlache Strait, however, we passed close by several icebergs, the intense pure blue of whose wave-carved grottoes reminded me of my introduction to Antarctica. Midway along the strait the *Hero* turned into a channel between Anvers and Brabant islands, following the west shore of Brabant to a bay under Mt. Parry. Here the bottom dredge was lowered and dragged for half an hour, for the purpose of obtaining information on the diurnal habits of certain Antarctic fishes. The trawls were to be repeated every six hours for a twenty-four-hour period. Between trawls, the ship was anchored in an ice-walled cove, the terminus of several glaciers that originated near the summits of mile-high mountains. Tumbling over rocky shoulders and sweeping through lower mountain valleys towards the sea, these rivers of ice sheered off abruptly, as though halting poised before the leap to their own destruction. Swirling vapors that had concealed the mountain tops lifted at sunset to give a fleeting glimpse of rosy peaks before night and snow closed in.

For the midnight trawl the ship was floodlit, thereby attracting dozens of Wilson's petrels. They settled on deck, entered the bridge through the open door, flew into the fo'c's'le, and fell into open empty crates. When daylight came, all but one of them flew away. Finding the bird that remained still at rest on netting in the forward storage room, I picked it up and held it, firmly at first, so that it could not escape. After fluttering vainly and weakly, uttering faint peeps, it settled down, resting motionless on my palm while I carried it out on deck, all the while stroking its head and back. With its wide webbed feet spread untrembling across my fingers, the bird was alert and clearly unafraid, turning its small head to look about. The delicate black bill was hooked at the tip, and tubular nostrils extended along half the length of its upper mandible—a characteristic of all tubenosed swimmers. I extended one long swallowlike wing and the petrel did not protest. Then, without warning, it raised both wings, fluttered away over the deck, and was gone out onto the sea.

From time to time, while the trawling continued, Antarctic terns circled the *Hero* in groups. Where they came from is not possible to say, since the shore of Brabant Island was almost totally covered with snow and ice and thus appeared to offer no suitable nesting sites.

By the second morning the clouds had cleared away, and in the afternoon, when the *Hero* returned to Palmer, Neumayer Strait was transformed. Hard, sharp sunlight and crystal air had dispersed the gloom of the passage out; now all was sparkling and bright. A day later the *Hero* set out again, once more in fine weather, for Deception Island, where there was to be further dredging for invertebrate specimens. She followed the same course through Neumayer Strait, where waters of a glassy calm, uniformly distributed between chunks of ice, mirrored the slopes of snow and rock and scree that rose on either side. In Gerlache Strait many small icebergs littered the surface, and flitting in and out among them were hundreds of Wilson's petrels feeding on plankton. Thanks to the clear and windless atmosphere, we moved through a blue world such as I had not seen before in Antarctica. The light from the azure sky, the darker blue of the sea, and the blue of shadows both light and dark, set off by white snow and small areas of black rock, were all-enveloping. Even those areas that appeared to contrast with what surrounded them turned out on closer examination to have a predominantly blue tint, apparently because much of the color other than blue had been filtered out or scattered by the water vapor in the atmosphere, and by the ice and snow on the land. The effect was of being submerged in a sea more ethereal and transparent than the true submarine environment, and therefore without its oppressive darkness.

By eight that evening, with Deception Island visible on the horizon, the sea was a boundless, unruffled sheet of undulating porcelain. Reflected in the polished blue and gray of its surface were the green of the horizon, the brownish smudge of distant clouds, and the yellowing sun as it shone on the peaks of Trinity Island—lobed, discrete, ephemeral reflected images like the patterns in oil, endlessly appearing, re-forming, and vanishing. How uncharacteristic all this was of the turbulent Antarctic Ocean!

We passed a few scattered chinstrap penguins floating unperturbed, their white throats gleaming in the setting sun, the ripples spreading in circles as they repeatedly dipped their beaks into the water. Wilson's petrels following the ship circled like swallows over a meadow, rising and sinking, pausing to flutter and touch the enameled surface with their large webbed feet, stirring up ripples of their own in the calm water. After the sun had set, its bluish porcelain gave way to a pinkish tint, mirroring filmy clouds that had gathered in a diffuse band above the eastern horizon, a chromatic counterpart to the green, yellow, and orange of the western afterglow.

That night the *Hero* anchored in Whaler's Bay within Deception Island lagoon, across from the Argentine station. Abandoned since the most recent volcanic eruption, the station has been unmanned for several years. In the morning I was ferried over for a look at it. I climbed from the cinder beach several hundred feet up the crater's side. Although no eruption had occurred on this side of the caldera for some time, all the rocks were volcanic and appeared to be of recent origin. I ascended a talus of cinders, ash, and scoria gullied by streams from melting snow high on the crater's rim. The water was beginning to freeze in thin, brittle sheets, glazing the stones and trapping white pockets of air. Black basaltic boulders and sulphur-yellow lumps of pumice were strewn about. The slope gradually leveled, to rise more steeply towards a maroon-colored wall of consolidated ash that rimmed the crater. The steep part of the slope was so extensively gullied that it looked unstable and would have been difficult to climb. Having decided against the attempt to reach the red wall, I followed a contour across a wide ravine to another talus, similar to the one by which I had come up. This proved a difficult traverse: the ravine was steeper than it had appeared at first, and was grooved by a series of narrow, boulder-filled gullies. This stony pavement would have presented no difficulty had its components been firmly fixed, but because they rested on ice, which underlay the entire area, they were disconcertingly unstable. As stones large and small gave way under the slightest pressure, they slid downhill, carrying still others with them. I felt my way across, mainly on hands and knees, not knowing when I might become part of a rock slide. Though I reached the other side without mishap, it was only after many close calls; at any moment I expected to see my camera case go tumbling down the mountain in a rocky avalanche. The second talus proved to be a ridge that dropped off on one side into a secondary crater. A blue lake lay cradled in volcanic rock at the bottom, kept from freezing by subterranean heat.

Back on the shore, I walked along the cinder beach to where volcanic deposits rose once more in a perpendicular cliff of reddish ash, much the same as the one I had tried to reach from the top of the talus. Scattered at the foot of this cliff and over the slopes leading to it were more sulphur-yellow boulders which had fallen from a pumice layer above the cliff. Such discontinuities between strata of different composition are typical of volcanic formations.

The Zodiac ride back to the *Hero*, which was trawling on the opposite side of the lagoon, against a stiff wind made the going unpleasantly wet. Although Zodiacs are reputed to be unsinkable and can land under almost any conditions on any kind of shore, in a choppy sea they become murderously uncomfortable.

In the evening the *Hero* steamed along a northerly course to enter Bransfield Strait. Trawling for krill, at different depths so as to obtain information on the diurnal benthic migration of these shrimplike organisms, continued all night. We returned in the early morning to Whaler's Bay, and after breakfast three of us who had slept through the night went ashore. Geothermal energy escaping through vents in the cinder beach produced steam, considerably warming the water in the vicinity. The life around the abandoned whaling station was exceptionally varied. Black-backed gulls rested in the water near the beach; a group of molting gentoo penguins had gathered on a snowbank above it; Weddell seals basked on the cinders, a solitary fur seal among them; and a flock of juvenile blue-eyed shags swam close inshore. When the shags entered the warm water they began to flap their wings vigorously, beating the surface and raising spray with a lot of splashing. I had never seen cormorants behave in this way, and it occurred to me that, unaccustomed to warm water, they were actually flapping to keep cool. After a few minutes of this, they flew off and settled down on the beach.

At 7:30 the *Hero* weighed anchor and left Port Foster—the official name of the lagoon—for another night of trawling. She circled Deception Island to the south and headed west, on a following wind, into the sun as it set in a blaze of yellow light. I watched in vain for the legendary green flash. The night air chilled rapidly, and I soon went below.

Early the next day I was awakened by the rolling of the ship, in striking contrast to the calm of the night before, and I supposed our course had taken us into the open ocean to the west of Anvers Island. But the change was due entirely to the weather. Low dark clouds formed a dense overcast, dramatically replacing the sunny skies of the last three days, and a strong wind was blowing. Our course was carrying us towards the Melchior Islands in Dallmann Bay, between Brabant and Anvers islands. This is a group of small, jagged islands on which the Argentine government had built a base (since dismantled) during the International Geophysical Year. As the *Hero* sailed into the narrow navigable passage between them, the sense of foreboding brought by the shifting storm clouds, which now cut off the upper reaches of the islands from view, was intensified by the spires of black rock that projected ominously from the water, and by the precarious balance in the fissured cliffs of ice whose collapse appeared imminent. Still without slackening, the ship rushed on into the gloom, inspiring confidence that she could successfully evade an unseen Scylla or Charybdis. During our passage the threatening atmosphere was relieved by a momentary break in the clouds, through which a shaft of light illuminated a high icefield.

By midafternoon the *Hero* was back at Palmer Station, where she refueled for the last cruise of the year, to Marguerite Bay south of the Antarctic Circle. I had dinner at the station and went to bed early. Snow fell intermittently all night, and by morning a gale was blowing from the east. We cast off at eight for Lemaire Channel south of Bismarck Strait. This channel, a rift in the Graham Coast of the Antarctic Peninsula that separates Booth Island from the mainland, was narrow and deep; on either side its walls rose almost vertically from the water, and locked into every ravine and col was a deeply fissured cascade of ice. These hanging glaciers appeared so near the verge of generating huge ice falls that to cruise under them at such close range, though unavoidable in the narrow passage, seemed full of risk. Even if a vessel escaped being directly engulfed by an avalanche, the waves thus produced would have dashed it against the cliffs. No ice fall occurred during the *Hero*'s passage, but the quantities of drifting ice in the channel showed that such occurrences were rare.

Traveling south from Lemaire Channel, we passed many small islands, large numbers of them capped with snow. Icebergs, free-floating or trapped and grounded, were numerous in the maze of shoals and reefs among the islands. The weathered and melting snowbanks overhanging the rocky shore were stained yellow, green, and red by algae, which gave a soiled look such as might be encountered near an industrial plant in winter—but one which from an esthetically detached point of view was in fact pleasing.

The sun broke through the clouds to the north, giving the Anvers Island mountains an amber glaze and backlighting the Argentine Islands, nearer by, with a warm glow. No hue was overwhelmed by any other, but each maintained its identity—the blues and purples against the yellows and oranges and pinks. This phenomenon is attributable to the clear air and to the low angle of sunlight in polar regions. Threading along an intricate passage among these resplendently colored islands, the *Hero* dropped anchor at a United Kingdom base where with some of the crew, Bill Fraser and I went ashore to pay a social call and drink some English ale, and to pick up the mail from the base.

We departed the Argentines at 2:30 for Adelaide Island, following the outer route where the ship met the full force of the winds and waves of the Bellingshausen Sea. Outside of Renaud, one of the Biscoe Islands group, the Antarctic ocean was rough, with long swells coming from two directions. A forty-knot gale blew up from the south, clearing the sky. The sea was a deep blue-black streaked with foam and spindrift and speckled with the white, semicircular crests of breaking waves. The *Hero* pitched and rolled heavily, taking a lot of water over the bow. Water squirted through the hawser pipes at each plunge.

Soon after we left the Argentine Islands, the sea was empty of icebergs. Birds, however, had increased in number and variety, for we were now on the edge of the polar feeding grounds. I saw several black-browed albatrosses, all juveniles; flocks of southern fulmars looking like dirty gulls; and snow petrels that followed the ship in company with groups of spotted black and white cape pigeons.

We ran south all night and much of the next day, coasting along twenty-five miles off the shores of Adelaide Island to Marguerite Bay. From the southern tip of Adelaide to Alexander Island, which we could see in the evening light as a faint orange and black sawtooth band on the horizon, the bay is 110 miles wide. At sunset southwest of Adelaide Island two bottom trawls were made in four hundred fathoms of water. The *Hero* loafed around all night, with one engine shut down, since at daylight we were to take on board two glacial geologists for the U.S. Geological Survey who had been collecting ice cores on the island, and who were waiting at the British base on its tip, which is west of Cape Alexander.

I was on the bridge soon after sunrise. The wind had greatly diminished but the sky was overcast with cumulostratus clouds, patches of blue peeking through them. A yellow stripe on the eastern horizon indicated where the sun had recently risen, illuminating the tops of the clouds and showing through as a rose tint wherever the cloud cover was thin. During the first hours of daylight the clouds gradually turned yellow.

Since the sea was too rough to permit the geologists to board at the unsheltered landing, we proceeded on around Cape Alexander and north along the east shore of Adelaide Island to Ryder Bay. Glaciers flowed from all the mountains surrounding this bay, cascading down every slope and lining the shore with ice except for one point of land where a scant acre of bare yellow rock was exposed. A fleet of icebergs calved from the land-born ice were floating there—huge, pinnacled and turreted ships and less commanding monitors whose low profile and smooth, grooved decks bespoke an evolution by capsizing and an age greater than that of their towering companions. The birth of an iceberg of glacial origin is a process of melting and of adjustment in its center of gravity to a stable position directly beneath the center of buoyancy. When as a result of underwater melting and the eroding action of waves this center of gravity is displaced upward, the iceberg loses its stability, rolling over into a new position, from which the relation between the two centers is re-established. After such a readjustment an iceberg oscillates until the released energy is absorbed by friction with the water; the more massive the berg, the greater the potential energy that must be dissipated and thus the longer it continues to rock. The eroded bottom now becomes the top, exhibiting all the features of ice long exposed to water at or near the melting point—a surface that is rounded, ribbed, and smooth. These surfaces often appear glazed, and shine in the sun with a specular brightness.

During the several bottom trawls that were carried out in Ryder Bay, the *Hero* passed close to many bergs. Some of those that had been recently overturned, with their curved and polished contours, suggested the furrowed white throats of rorqual whales floating upside down in the water. Azure caverns that had eroded deep into the ice mass at the waterline of the younger, turreted bergs glowed like immense jewels in the filtered and reflected sunlight. Adélie penguins that had somehow climbed the slippery surfaces gawked at us nervously from the high vantage of their positions.

From Ryder Bay the *Hero* proceeded north, passing the new British station under construction on Stone-house Bay, and proceeding out into the channel that divides Adelaide Island from the mainland. With her engines throttled down she marked time before beginning an evening trawl, and when that was completed she turned south again in the twilight for Cape Alexander. Another night trawl was made south of Adelaide Island, and on the morning of March 4 we took the two Americans from the old British base on board.

I was up soon after the sun had reappeared in the southeast. Since we were south of the Antarctic Circle, the sun had not actually set but had been obscured by clouds in the southern sky. As we ran west from the southern tip of Adelaide Island, a narrow strip of sky over the distant mainland was the only clear area. Through that strip the sun shone briefly, a bright yellow ball illuminating the undersides of clouds to the east. The mountains of Adelaide and the mainland far in the distance were silhouetted in aerial perspective, range behind range against the band of gold.

As we headed north to return to Palmer, the weather continued to worsen. The north wind gathered strength as the *Hero* sailed into the eye of the storm, pitching with increased violence as the waves built up, until the sea was streaked with ribbons of foam. Spray over the bow was continuous; and now and again, when the ship encountered a series of exceptionally large seas not synchronous with her natural period of oscillation, she would plunge deep into the advancing front of the first sea, raising green water onto her foredeck, and slap joltingly down on the next, fanning sheets of water to either side. Clouds of spray enveloped the entire ship all the way aft to the fantail, and rattled on the windows of the bridge. The violent plunges continued as the ship passed through a series of large waves between which the troughs were so deep that their foamy surfaces were untouched by the gale.

As on the trip south, many species of petrels flew past and around the ship. The birds seemed actually to relish the storm. Rain in the morning had turned to snow by noon and to a full-scale blizzard by four o'clock. Visibility gradually decreased, down to just over a hundred yards, and the ship's speed was reduced because of the imminence of icebergs.

The next morning, once again, I was on the bridge at six. A considerable swell was running but the wind had died down, and the first light of day had begun to penetrate the low gray clouds, revealing an equally cheerless, colorless sea and sky. Rain was falling, the windshield wipers flicking back and forth across the wheelhouse windows. The only lights were a small red spot over the chart table and a glow from the Simrad radar. The first mate was on watch, and Captain Lenie was bent over the radar screen. The *Hero* was approaching a nest of icebergs large and small, which showed on the radar as bright blips and patches. I understood from conversation between the captain and the mate that during the night the ship had been turned back and hove to so as to avoid navigating among the icebergs in the dark. Visibility was less than a mile. The nearest bergs loomed up out of the mist like ghosts, the intrinsic blue tint of glacial ice just faintly visible as we passed. The spray from the waves breaking against the largest of these ice islands, and the zone of encircling foam, had both been colored yellow by a prolific bloom of plankton. The low-profiled smaller icebergs, smoothed and rounded by the sea, wallowed in the swell like pale sea monsters, sinking and rising, their backs streaming with water. The swell subsided as we moved towards Matha Strait, which separates Adelaide from Lavoisier Island, and from there into quieter, ice-free waters. As night closed in the *Hero* slowed and was eventually allowed to drift with the engines shut down. Through the deepening gloom a solitary snow petrel, of immaculate purity except for its black eye, could be seen gliding over the steely water on stiff, unmoving wings.

I was awakened at five by the sounds of the ship getting under way, bound this time for Prospect Point on the mainland of the Antarctic Peninsula. Through heavy clouds the light of the coming day was just beginning to show, a streak of pale yellow. On either side of our course, small icebergs and cakes of ice were becoming numerous—delicately tinted blue and white, intricately sculptured, filigreed, and fragile in the dim light of early morning. The impression of a changeless, enduring state, of a retarding in the flow of time, was fortified by the glassy stillness of the sea as it reflected each subtle shape. It appeared as though, once created, these frozen works of nature were no longer subject to change.

As we pushed deeper into the sheltered coastal waters towards Prospect Point, the ice became more closely packed and the ship had to be steered from the upper bridge. After we anchored at the point, while the crew and most of the passengers went ashore to explore the abandoned British outpost, Bill Fraser and I went off by Zodiac. Our first visit was to a nearby island notable for a massive arch of ice extending like a flying buttress from the front of a glacier onto a gravel bar. We next visited a group of small low islands called the Minnows, where shags, penguins, and gulls were nesting, each colony scrupulously segregated on a separate islet. On one island, Adélie penguins—all of them molting adults—stood about in lethargic clusters, waiting patiently for the time when a new coat of insulating plumage would permit them to go back into the water. The muddy ground all about them was thickly strewn with feather quills.

In the middle of the afternoon we weighed anchor and headed west to Grandidier Channel, from which our course led northward towards the Argentine Islands. The open water of the channel was littered with ice floes, small icebergs, and ice cakes of all sizes and shapes, some white, others pale blue, and a few colored a deep ultramarine. As we turned into Grandidier Channel we approached a very large tabular iceberg, for years a wanderer on the polar seas that had finally drifted towards the shelter of these Antarctic bays. The history of its erratic voyaging could be read in its grooved and craggy façade, whose pillared arches offered a glimpse into a blue, unknowable labyrinth of halls and galleries, the haunt of seals and fishes.

Golden light tinged the crests of the mountains on the mainland and the islands to the east of the channel for more than an hour while the sun slipped below a horizon, concealed behind a bank of clouds. The effects produced by stratified clouds lying low and dark across the lower mountain slopes and above the illuminated peaks were dramatic.

The last of a series of trawls, which went on throughout the night, was conducted at dawn just south of the entrance to Lemaire Passage. The mountains on either side were lost in clouds, obscuring all but the lower ends of the glaciers as we steamed through. Then, suddenly, all was bright sunlight as we emerged into a strait cluttered with glistening icebergs; wispy vapors encircled the summit of Mt. Français and the mountains of Wiencke Island. Shortly after noon on March 7, we docked once more at Palmer Station.

The party that spontaneously evolved that evening at the station was a farewell by those few who were staying behind, a little sad and envious, to those of us who, with anticipation tempered by regret, would be leaving Antarctica. Since loading, provisioning, and fueling were to occupy all the next day, Bill Fraser suggested a last Zodiac trip to Litchfield and Humble islands—the last for him too since such trips are not permitted during the winter. On Litchfield, while Bill was searching out his banded birds, another scientist and I set out to circumnavigate the island. The brash and sea ice were so thick on the outer side that we had to turn back, but where there had been open water shortly before, ice had moved in, completely covering the sea and obliging us to force a way through, ramming the cakes at the risk of shearing a propeller pin. Fortunately the laminated rubber and fabric construction of the Zodiac was so tough and resilient that it was not damaged. Our day ended with an uneventful last visit to Humble Island.

The *Hero* was scheduled to depart for Ushuaia in the evening of the next day, March 9, with a stop at Deception Island for inspection before crossing the Drake Passage. Early in the afternoon the *Gedania*, a two-masted Marconi-rigged auxiliary schooner from Gdansk in Poland, motored into Arthur Harbor and tied up alongside the *Hero*. After a brief exchange of courtesies she sailed for the Argentine Islands.

The *Hero* cast off at 5:30 for Almirante Brown, the Argentine station in Paradise Harbor, to pick up mail for Ushuaia. While we were crossing Bismarck Strait, a strange blue light appeared below the clouds where glaciers of the mainland showed between mountain peaks—an eerie luminescence produced in some way by light from the sky filtering through high, thin clouds and illuminating the ice sheet. As the sun sank westward the undersides of low clouds turned to a yellow-brown color under the graying blue of higher cloud layers.

The fjordlike passage to Almirante Brown was filled with icebergs, but the *Hero* wove her way among them at full speed. In daylight the channel would have been spectacular. We arrived in darkness, however, the ship's searchlights picking out the icebergs one by one as they loomed up ahead, lighting them to a dazzling whiteness as they rushed past on either side. We left the Argentine station within half an hour of our arrival.

At sunrise Trinity Island was off the starboard bow, with Deception Island dead ahead. Early in the afternoon we anchored again in Whaler's Bay, and an hour and a half later were under way for a social rendezvous with the British ship *Bransfield* at Half Moon Island, the site of an abandoned Argentine station on McFarlane Strait. Just beyond a chain of rocks inside Renier Point, on the way to our rendezvous, was a large grounded iceberg, its smoothly rounded contours showing that it had been recently overturned. The most remarkable thing about it, however, was its translucent, bright green color, like a huge piece of gemstone jade. A horizontal band of yellowish green blending with the dominant color encircled it midway up its sloping sides. The first explanation for this unusual color that came to mind was that some form of plant life was dispersed through the ice. The *British Antarctic Pilot* says that black and green icebergs which have been reported in the Weddell Sea are thought to be of morainic origin, owing their color to the incorporation of finely ground mineral matter. For black icebergs the explanation was plausible, but for a green one the unlikely incorporation of a mineral such as copper would have to be presumed. Even granting such a possibility, the result would be opaque rather than translucent ice. Therefore the most logical explanation for the color of the grounded iceberg seemed to be the incorporation of some form of phytoplankton or algaelike organisms.

At six on March 11, the morning after our visit to the *Bransfield*, the *Hero* was under way, running northeast to Nelson Strait between Robert and Nelson islands. Thousands of penguins, mostly of the chinstrap species, were porpoising along in shoals or flocks through the tide rip, easily keeping abreast of the ship as she pitched heavily in the short seas. As we emerged from the straight—the compass set for Horn Island, five hundred miles out across the "terrible" Drake Passage—I was leaving Antarctica for good. All that night and all through the day and night that followed, we ran north, rolling sluggishly in the trough of the sea. At 9:00 A.M. on March 13 we came in sight of Tierra del Fuego.

INDEX

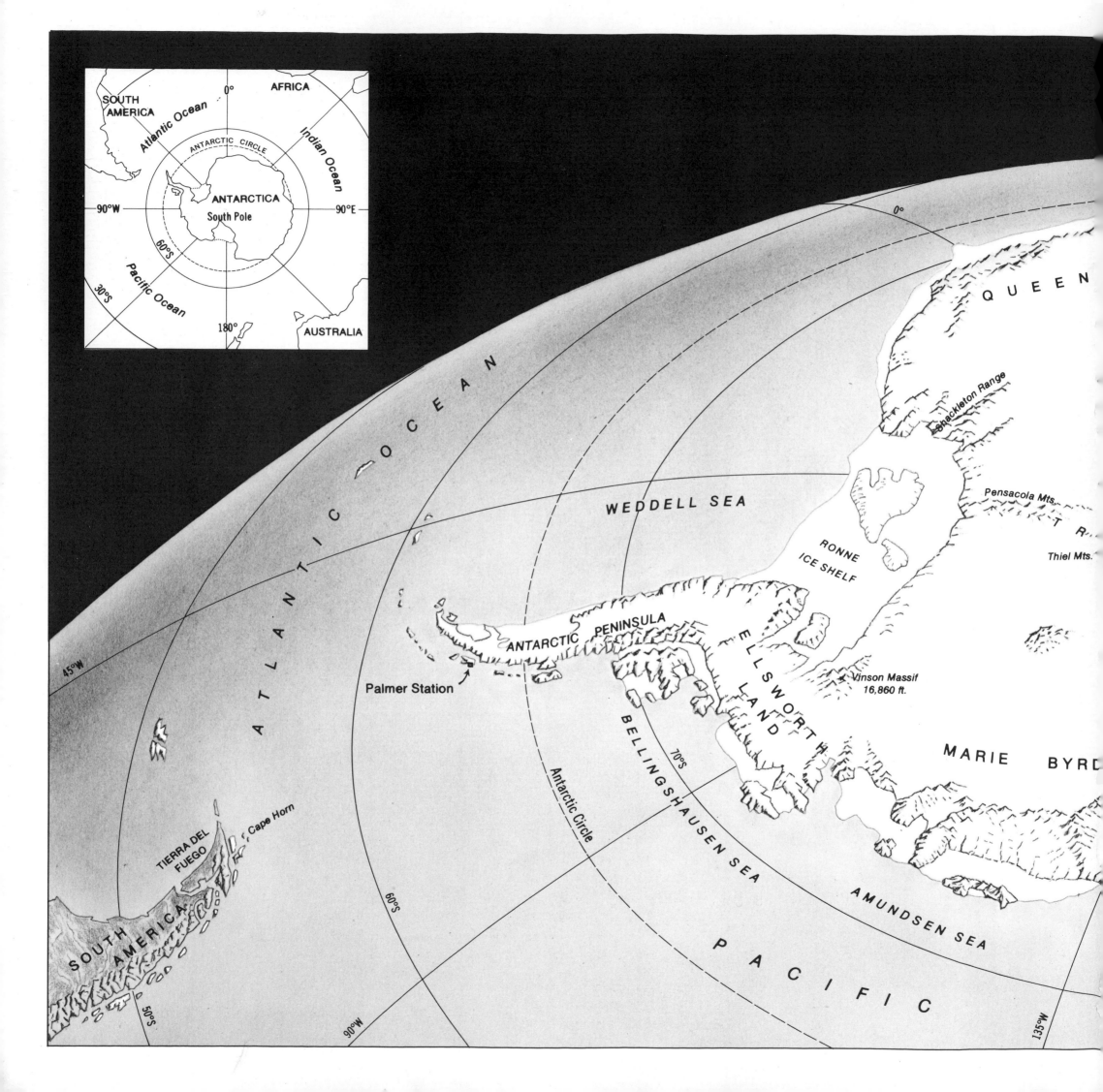